LIFE
MANAGEMEN .

LIFE MANAGEMENT

SKILLS FOR BUSY PEOPLE

BRENDA L. WALTERS, B.C.S.W.

SANDRA L. McKEE
DeVry Institute of Technology

Prentice Hall, Upper Saddle River, New Jersey 07458

Library of Congress Cataloging-in-Publication Data

Walters, Brenda L., (date)
Life management : skills for busy people / Brenda L. Walters.
Sandra L. McKee
p. cm.
Includes bibliographical references.
ISBN 0-13-227539-2 (pbk.)
1. Success—Psychological aspects. 2. Self-actualization (Psychology) 3. Goal (Psychology) 4. Motivation (Psychology)
I. McKee, Sandra L., (date). II. Title.
BF637.S8W313 1996
158—dc20 96-18516
CIP

Acquisition Editor: Elizabeth Sugg
Editorial/production supervision, interior design, and electronic page makeup: Mary Araneo
Buyer: Ed O'Dougherty
Cover director: Jayne Conte

Simon & Schuster/A Viacom Company
Upper Saddle River, New Jersey 07458

Printed in the United States of America

10 9 8 7 6 5 4 3 2 1

ISBN 0-13-227539-2

Prentice-Hall International (UK) Limited, *London*
Prentice-Hall of Australia Pty. Limited, *Sydney*
Prentice-Hall Canada Inc., *Toronto*
Prentice-Hall Hispanoamericana, S.A., *Mexico*
Prentice-Hall of India Private Limited, *New Delhi*
Prentice-Hall of Japan, Inc., *Tokyo*
Simon & Schuster Asia Pte. Ltd., *Singapore*
Editora Prentice-Hall do Brasil, Ltda., *Rio de Janeiro*

CONTENTS

PREFACE XI
To the Instructor or Seminar Leader xii

UNIT ORGANIZATION XIII
Where To Focus Your Efforts Chart xiv

TO THE READER XV

ABOUT THE AUTHORS XVII

ACKNOWLEDGMENTS XIX

I STAGE ONE: ASSESS THE SITUATION FOR CHANGE 1

1 BUILDING THE FOUNDATION: A FORMULA FOR SUCCESS 3

Understanding the Formula 5
Personal Life Management Skill #1: Define Your Dream 9
Personal Life Management Plan Step #1: Define Your Dream 10

2 REALIZING YOUR POTENTIAL THROUGH CHANGE 11

Dealing with Change 13
Personal Life Management Skill #1: Find Areas of Discomfort 19
Quick Tips to Make Change Easy 19
Personal Life Management Skill #2: Make a Commitment 20

Personal Life Management Skill #3: Visualize Change 20
Personal Life Management Skill #4: Practice Change Behaviors 22
Personal Life Management Plan Step #2 23

UNIT I PROGRESS CHECK AND AFFIRMATION 25

II STAGE TWO: GATHER NECESSARY TOOLS 27

3 ORGANIZING TIME AND TASKS 29

Why We Have Trouble with Organization 30
Thinking Styles 30
Skills Development 33
Saying "No" 34
Personal Life Management Skill #1: Prioritize Necessary Track 38
Personal Life Management Plan Step #2: Securing Resources 39
Time Just Gets Away 41
Too Many Things To Do 42
Personal Life Management Skill #3: Completing the Tasks 42
Personal Life Management Plan Step #3 43
Time and Task Organization Sheet 44

4 GATHERING INFORMATION AS LIFELONG LEARNING 47

Finding Information 47
Information Processing 50
Active Listening 52
Personal Life Management Plan Skill #1: Become an Active Listener 54
Inter-Active Reading 55
Barriers To Speed and Comprehension 57
Personal Life Management Plan Skill #2: Use Inter-Active Reading 60
Personal Life Management Plan Step #4 61

UNIT II PROGRESS CHECK AND AFFIRMATION 63

III STAGE THREE: DEVELOP CRITICAL SKILLS 65

5 USING CONSTRUCTIVE COMMUNICATION 67

Resolving Negative Patterns 67
Building Constructive Communication 72
Personal Life Management Skill #1: Eliminate Negative Talk 72
Personal Life Management Skill #2: Adopt Constructive Style 74
Personal Life Management Skill #3: Build a Constructive Environment 76
Personal Life Management Plan Step #5 77

6 REPLACING WORRYING WITH PROBLEM SOLVING 79

Learned Worry Styles 79
Sources of Worry 80
Using Critical Thinking to Isolate the Problem 82
Personal Life Management Skill #1: Thinking Creatively to Generate Solutions 85
Personal Life Management Skill #2: Generate Solutions 85
Analyzing to Weed Out the Least Workable 86
Personal Life Management Skill #3: Weed Out the Least Workable 87
Acting to Implement Your Choice 88
Personal Life Management Skill #4: Implement Your Choice 88
Congratulating Yourself to Affirm Your Achievement 89
Personal Life Management Skill #5: Congratulate Yourself 89
Personal Life Management Plan Step #5 90

7 CONFRONTING CONFLICT 91

Conflicting Needs as a Source of Conflict 91
Approaches to Conflict 92
Personal Life Management Skill #1: Handle Emotions 97
Personal Life Management Skill #2: Listen to Detail 98
Personal Life Management Skill #3: Assert Your Needs 99
Personal Life Management Skill #4: Acknowledge Other's Needs 100

Personal Life Management Skill #5: Focus on Issues 101
Personal Life Management Skill #6: Find Mutual Solutions 102
Personal Life Management Plan Step #7 104

UNIT III PROGRESS CHECK AND AFFIRMATION 105

IV STAGE FOUR: BUILD EFFECTIVE RELATIONSHIPS 107

8 SELF-NURTURING 109

Body Needs 112
Personal Life Management Skill #1: Take Care of Your Body Needs 113
Breaks 113
Personal Life Management Skill #2: Take a Break 114
Growth 115
Personal Life Management Skill #3: Challenge for Growth 115
Privacy 116
Personal Life Management Skill #4: Create Privacy 116
Finances 117
Personal Life Management Skill #5: Manage Finances Responsibly 118
Affiliations 119
Personal Life Management Skill #6: Form Meaningful Affiliations 119
Limits 120
Personal Life Management Skill #7: Observe Limits 121
Personal Life Management Plan Step #8 122

9 DEVELOPING SUSTAINING RELATIONSHIPS 123

Draining Relationships 123
Sustaining Relationships 125
Building Better Relationships 128
Supportive Listening 128
Personal Life Management Skill #1: Use Supportive Listening 129
Voicing Needs 130
Personal Life Management Skill #2: Voice Needs 130
Handling Conflicting Needs 131

Personal Life Management Skill #3: Handle Conflicting Needs 132
Re-thinking rejection 133
Personal Life Management Skill #4: Re-thinking Rejection 133
Personal Life Management Plan Step #9 134

10 CULTIVATING INTIMATE RELATIONSHIPS 135

Ineffective Relationships 136
Intimate Relationships 139
Increasing Intimacy in Relationships 141
Know Yourself 141
Personal Life Management Skill #1: Know Yourself 142
Follow the Rules 143
Personal Life Management Skill #2: Follow the Rules 144
Be Persistent 145
Personal Life Management Skill #3: Be Persistent 146
Personal Life Management Plan Step #10 147

UNIT IV PROGRESS CHECK AND AFFIRMATION 149

V STAGE FIVE: IMPLEMENT PERSONAL AND PROFESSIONAL PLAN 151

11 ACHIEVING PROFESSIONAL GROWTH 153

Select a Goal 158
Personal Life Management Skill #1: Set a Goal 159
Talk It Up To Yourself 159
Personal Life Management Skill #2: Talk It Up To Yourself 160
Revive Your Curiosity 160
Personal Life Management Skill #3: Revive Your Curiosity 161
Elevate Your Goat To a Daily Priority 162
Personal Life Management Skill #4: Elevate Your Goal 162
Take Advantage of Opportunities 163
Personal Life Management Skill #5: Take Opportunity 164
Charge Ahead with Confidence 165
Personal Life Management Skill #6: Charge Ahead 166
Have a Heart 166
Personal Life Management Skill #7: Have a Heart 167
Personal Life Management Plan Step #11 168

12 IMPLEMENTING YOUR PERSONAL LIFE MANAGEMENT PLAN 169

Implementing Your Plans 170
Continuing Development Using Your Personal Life Management Plan 177
Personal Life Management Plan Entry #12 178

UNIT V PROGRESS CHECK AND AFFIRMATION 179

PERSONAL LIFE MANAGEMENT PLAN SUMMARY 181

PERSONAL LIFE MANAGER CERTIFICATE 183

PRACTICE EXERCISES 185

CAREER PLANNING SUPPLEMENT—BUILDING A RESUME 195

SUGGESTED READING 201

PREFACE

This book is the combined effort of a therapist who works with individuals in both hospital and outpatient settings and a business professor/consultant who coaches both college students and industrial clients in the area of professional development. It has grown out of our experiences with the needs and successes of these people. Therefore, we designed this as a guide to actively assist others who want to make a significant change in their lives.

Unlike many personal/professional development books that drown readers in theory or detailed examples of problems, *Life Management : A Guide for Busy People* will present the ABC's of change toward a life without struggle. This book will help readers develop a Personal Life Management Plan. It will also give tools for goal fulfillment that are easily utilized on a minute-by-minute, day-by-day basis.

The skills taught in this book are plainly stated and easily understood. The approach takes into account the many demands on busy people's lives and is a workable plan for even the most overtaxed person. We have carefully tried to address most of the skills necessary for laying a good interpersonal foundation for business or personal life. Topics such as goal setting, positive communication, conflict resolution, self-nurturing, time management, and career planning help readers discover the power of using new skills to become change agents for themselves.

From a theoretical perspective, the book takes a behavioral approach which will help readers move in a stepwise manner. The purpose is to provide a stand-alone guide for individuals in a collegiate, industrial, or therapeutic environment.

The formula presented in this book is built on what real people deal with on a daily basis. We walk the readers through the change process and support them until the new behaviors become an unconscious habit. A strength of the approach is its regular engagement of readers in activities that reinforce the ideas presented. Thus, reinforcement of the new behaviors occurs instantly.

TO THE INSTRUCTOR OR SEMINAR LEADER

All concepts presented are paired with case examples from all walks of life to increase readers' identification with the problems and solutions discussed. At the end of each chapter is a summary/restatement of the **Personal Life Management Plan's** main points for that chapter. At the end of each unit is an encouraging statement from the authors affirming the progress so far and urging continuation of the work begun in the unit.

Activities are short but require thought and creativity as readers develop a plan for changing their lives. These activities are in several formats:

Assessment activities, where readers examine their own situations with a critical eye, and chronicle events, attitudes, and knowledge that pertain to chapter concepts.

Personal Life Management Plan skill development, where readers apply the chapter ideas to developing a plan for change in their own lives.

Practice exercises (in the back of the book), where readers apply chapter ideas to situations offered for practice. These include applications that encourage recall and application of concepts, and also situation analyses that invite critical thinking.

This material has been tested with over 300 college students and 150 business personnel. The approach, however, utilized by the authors in their daily interactions with students and clients, has been proven successful over and over.

Brenda Walters, BCSW
Sandra McKee, M.A.T.

UNIT ORGANIZATION

Unit I consists of Chapters 1 and 2 in which readers have the opportunity to review their current situations and engage in goal setting in a guided and supported way.

Unit II, Chapters 3 and 4, offers a set of skills that readers will develop in order to begin changing their basic operating styles. These chapters include skill building in time management, communication, critical thinking, problem solving, and conflict management.

Unit III, Chapters 5, 6, and 7, includes skill building in positive communication, critical thinking, problem solving, and conflict management.

Unit IV, Chapters 8, 9, and 10, leads readers through improving their relationships in both their personal and professional lives. These chapters offer guidance in developing those interpersonal relationships which are necessary for a fulfilling life and for successful work interactions.

Unit V, Chapters 11 and 12, applies the concepts from throughout the book, as it gives readers the specifics for carrying out the principles in building a productive and satisfying career. These chapters help readers integrate what has been learned.

Critical Thinking challenges are integrated into each chapter to draw readers into analyzing a short case and applying the newly learned chapter skills in performing this analysis. These challenges are enclosed in boxes in each chapter and are noted by an icon.

Practice exercises occur at the end of the written text and are keyed to each chapter so that readers can perform a quick check on how well they are internalizing the concepts. There is also an important supplement about building a resume that can be utilized whenever readers or guides feel appropriate.

Where do you need to focus your efforts? The chart below will help you find the part of this book you need to review the most:

RESOURCES	Time	Time and task organization	Chapter 3	Goals, planning, prioritizing
	Material and facilities	Time and task organization	Chapter 3	Plans for securing materials
INTERPERSONAL	Participate as team member	Positive communication	Chapter 5	Avoiding negativity
	Exercises leadership	Conflict management	Chapter 7	Determine issues, mutual solutions
	Negotiates	Conflict management	Chapter 7	Listening skills resolution
INFORMATION	Acquires and evaluates info	Lifelong learning	Chapter 4-	Information search
	Organizes and maintains info	Active listening and interactive reading	Chapter 4	Taking notes for memory
SYSTEMS	Understands systems	Social and work environments	Chapter 2	Becoming a change agent
BASIC SKILLS	Reading	Active reading	Chapter 4	Pre-reading diagrams
	Listening	Interactive listening	Chapter 4	Pre-listening guides
THINKING SKILLS	Creative thinking	Critical thinking	Throughout each chapter	Critical thinking applications
	Decision making/ problem solving	Problem solving	Chapter 6	Solving personal and work problems
	Knowing how to learn	Preparing to read or listen	Chapter 4	Anticipating information needs
PERSONAL QUALITIES	Responsibility	Goal setting	Chapter 1	Defining life goals
	Responsibility	Respecting others' needs	Chapter 10	Build desirable relationships
	Self-esteem	Taking care of self	Chapter 8	Assessing and meeting own needs
	Sociability	Work/personal relationships	Chapter 9	Personal interaction rules
	Self-management	Develop life plan	Chapter 12 and throughout	Setting and monitoring Life Plan

To the Reader

In developing your **Personal Life Management Plan,** you will draw from your own internal resources; understand your values and directions; change old, ineffective thoughts; and develop a personalized set of strategies to take you toward the kind of life you would choose for yourself. If you are content with your life, this book will help you learn new skills to enhance what you are now experiencing. If you feel your life is frustrating and too often chaotic, then it will guide you out of that maze.

No one is able to remove all problems from life, so we must be realistic about what we want to accomplish. If you are uncomfortable with your life right now, that is good. A little discomfort moves us to change things to make them better. It makes us become motivated to seek a solution to the problems that plague us. As you read through this book, incorporate the techniques as you learn them. By doing this, you will develop a menu of workable options for your individual situation.

So, expect to put forth some effort in the beginning, until the new strategies become second nature. When this happens, you will begin to experience your desired effect. In this manner you will move steadily closer to your dream.

Finally, **reading this book will not change your life. But you, by incorporating the skills you will learn in this book, will change your life.**

Brenda Walters, BCSW
Sandra McKee, M.A.T.

About the Authors

Brenda Walters, M.S.W., B.C.S.W. is a licensed clinical social worker. She has a private practice, located at Methodist Psychiatric Pavilion in New Orleans, where she specializes in adult psychotherapy. Ms. Walters works with patients who are in the hospital as well as those seen on an outpatient basis. Additionally, she is the clinical director of the outpatient addictions program at the hospital. She overseas the treatment of individuals with a variety of types of addictions including duel disorders. Ms. Walters recently has focused much of her attention on gambling addictions and has spoken about the problems facing families both on a local basis and a national level. Ms. Walters has appeared on numerous radio and TV programs as well as being a featured speaker for corporations where she addresses personal growth and development skills.

Sandra McKee has spent most of her adult life assisting people with their personal and professional growth: from her early days as director of a therapeutic horseback riding program for handicapped children and adults to her current roles as college professor, professional development consultant, and motivational speaker. Today, McKee is a Senior Professor in the General Studies Department at DeVry Institute of Technology in Atlanta. She has spoken to groups as far distant as Hawaii, California, Vermont, Rhode Island, and Florida. Her teaching responsibilities include her favorite course—Motivation and Leadership—a professional development course that prepares college seniors for the challenges of the workplace. Her consulting work includes executive development coaching with senior managers as well as employee screening and training.

Acknowledgments

The authors wish to acknowledge all those who contributed to the development of this book: our clients, students, colleagues, peers, and families. All who participated in this process, either by testing the material, offering ideas, or reviewing drafts, have helped bring this project to its successful completion. We are grateful to all of you. For their comments on content, we would like to thank Dr. Ward Deutschman, Briarcliffe College; Edith Carlson-Abbey, Rice University; and Maris Roze, DeVry Institute of Technology.

In addition, we thank our own teachers over the years, those in the classrooms of higher learning and those in our daily lives, who took the time to share their wisdom with us. Much of this wisdom appears in this book.

I

STAGE ONE: ASSESS THE SITUATION FOR CHANGE

1 Building the Foundation

A Formula for Success

"I can't seem to get a grip on my life."
"I've struggled for so long."
"Things never go right for me."
"If only I could get a break."
"If only things would change for me."

Does any of this sound familiar? It should. You may have even said some of these things yourself. For certain, many people share your feelings. They suffer with despair, frustration, and helplessness in the face of rapid change. If you are feeling the same thing, you are in the company of a multitude of us who are searching for a path to successful living by learning self-development skills and by improving personal and work relationships.

The problem is that many of us see ourselves as having limited potential. We go through life with a minimum of effort because we have low expectations for our own success. In addition, we often lack the foundation skills to assist us in our development.

Our perception of our own potential should not be a limiting factor in our dreams for a good and happy life. It should free us to make those dreams happen! See how this sounds for a new approach:

When you make changes in your life and in your operating style, you change your potential.

Consider for a moment how powerful an idea this is. You can change your potential for success by changing small things in your present. Whatever you think the future holds in store for you, bad or good, you can alter that by doing some things differently today. In fact, that realization is so important, I would ask you to repeat it to yourself as the first step in choosing your own destiny.

By making changes in my life and my operating style, I change my potential.

If Hal sees himself as a "truck driver," he may never fulfill the dreams he has of being an owner-operator. But if he takes a business course, or works out a savings and investment plan, he can change for the better his prospects of owning his own rig and being independent.

This notion of altering your own potential has been proven time and again. If you study the lives of successful people, you will find that they always see themselves as having more "potential" than others, and more importantly, they act on that basis. As you change the way you relate to people and problems, to *act* in terms of your new potential, you will find more freedom in your choices of life direction.

The only barrier between you and the future you want is the past and the effect it is having on you now.

This chapter will begin to guide you in sifting through the old and ineffective operating styles you have picked up over the years. After you have sorted through the relics, you will be able to develop your own ***Personal Life Management Plan.*** This will be the formula for the changes that most people desperately want.

Clearly, over the years people need some basic formula from which to operate in order to build their lives into the dreams they choose. No one is born with the formula, nor is there any formal rite of passage in our society where we are handed the formula. Developing this formula, this plan, becomes an individual growth process. It is the basis, or foundation, on which you build your dream.

Though the formula is simple to understand, it will take a commitment on your part to follow through in the process that will make it work for you. As you utilize the formula, you will note that:

- It flows in a logical, stepwise manner.
- It requires no more effort than it takes to bemoan misfortune.
- And, no one will know what you are doing that is changing your life so dramatically.

In these pages you will be asked to define your own goals, look at your own issues, and come up with your own ***Personal Life Management Plan.*** And, at the end of the book you will be able to organize your plan to focus on any area of your life that is a problem. You will, in effect, have a blueprint for high performance.

The simple guidelines that we will give you will stay with you long after you have read this book and worked the exercises. Throughout this book you will find self-empowering ideas—ideas that will make you stop and think about your current life view and will invite you to consider a new outlook. These will appear in boldface print.

In addition, there will be many occasions for you to develop and **apply critical thinking skills.** These will occur in the form of assessment activities within the chapters and in practice exercises found at the end of the book. In these activities and exercises you will be asked to look at either your own life situation or at someone else's. Then, you will write your thoughts and make recommendations for action. By doing all these activities, you will practice the skills you are learning, and soon they will feel very natural to you as you apply them to your daily life.

What Do You Think?

Why would someone want to make changes in his or her life?

UNDERSTANDING THE FORMULA

Everything you say, do, and become begins with how you think. How you think becomes who you are. Up to this point, your life direction has probably, like most people's, been working largely at the unconscious level. You don't plan what you think or how you will react; you just do it. It's you and it's comfortable.

Or maybe it's not comfortable. Maybe the destiny you saw in the mirror this morning is not what you really want for yourself. But, how do you change destiny? It's a lot simpler than you might have expected. By examining patterns that are keeping your life on automatic pilot, by actively selecting , changing, and adding to them, you will be able to take control and steer yourself in a direction that will increase your success potential.

STEP 1: ASSESS YOUR SITUATION FOR CHANGE

By using a carefully guided search process, you will be able to discover the problem areas in your operating style and in your relationships. Whatever is interfering with your happiness can only be dealt with when you become aware of what the problem really is. By thoughtfully looking at where you are now, in relation to where you want to be, you will be making the first move toward improving the quality of your life.

After you have begun the examination process, you will have a clearer picture of the areas of your life or behaviors that need to be changed. Change is troublesome to most people. We resist it violently. We run from it, and we deny it is happening all around us. Eventually, though, we reluctantly give in to it.

Rather than look at areas of improvement, we stubbornly bury our heads in the sand, spend a lot of effort covering our weaknesses, and then sadly tell others, "That's just the way I am. Take it or leave it." It is almost as if we put our worst foot forward and dare people to greet us with love and understanding.

An excellent example of this is the hiring process. Many employers report that their experience in interviewing is not always positive. "People come in with a scowl on their faces and an attitude that says, 'You probably don't want to hire me anyway, so I'll save you the trouble.'" Consequently, these people become the chronically unemployed. They blame their lack of success on "the system" or "she just couldn't see my good points."

I guess not! Learning to assess who you really are and what you truly have to offer is a surprisingly difficult task for most people. In fact, it is so difficult for employers to find people who can clearly and positively describe their skills and professional character that they are resorting more and more to psychological and professional assessment testing to find good employees.

Taking control of your life then becomes a process of understanding yourself in terms of others: friends, co-workers, fellow students, spouses, children, and lovers.

If we don't like the way we are talked to, or treated, or cared for, then we have to accept some responsibility for making the changes necessary to get the treatment we want.

We can choose change that is effective and rewarding. Actually, changing certain aspects of our tone of voice, our dress, or even our posture can be enough to greatly improve the quality of our lives. But, we must decide that change is needed before we can take any steps toward a happier life.

STAGE 2: GATHER NECESSARY TOOLS

Once you decide to make a change, you must organize your life in a way that will allow you time for the work you must do. Any person who is pulled several different ways, by demands of work, family, school, and then, making life changes, has to begin the process with the necessary tools. Time management is a tool that is needed throughout life by most people.

A second tool that is required to ensure success in making changes is information. Many vehicles exist today that can help us find out what we need to know. We are all exposed to newspapers, books, magazines, computers, and experts in many fields. The Internet, CD-ROM information services, and databases with seemingly inexhaustable sources are available in public and college libraries as well as in hundreds of thousands of homes across the country. Information is a tool that becomes part of every task we do in our pursuit of a successful life.

STEP 3: DEVELOP CRITICAL SKILLS

Once you begin thinking differently, you will then need to **add new skills for a better operating style.** Your new skills will enhance the personality or character that defines you. Perhaps being better able to communicate, or solve personal or work problems will improve your life. Maybe you have difficulties with conflict. **Whatever your goal and whatever you may feel you lack, you can learn ways to handle life situations better.** In this way you will develop a positive self-image, and a successful life.

It will be necessary to learn a different, better approach to these situations. As you learn a new skill, you will need to practice it on a daily basis as many times as you can. Though it may feel unnatural at first (old ways die hard), the good news is that you will soon get accustomed to your better, and more effective, operating style. After a while, things will go better for you, and you will feel perfectly comfortable with the new behaviors.

It's like learning to ride a bike. At first you were afraid. Then you managed to do it, even though you were fearful. As you kept practicing, you got better and better. Pretty soon you were able to ride without holding on. You developed the skill of bike riding at an unconscious level, and to this day, you do not have to think of all the steps it takes to ride a bike. You just do it.

STEP 4: IMPROVE RELATIONSHIPS

As you get better at using your new skills, you will begin to use them to improve the relationships you have. There are all sorts of relationships that each of us is a part of, and none of them are simple. We have family, neighbors, co-workers, friends, acquaintances, all kinds of ways and levels of being involved with people.

Improving relationships just makes everything else in our lives go better. We often put up with unhealthy relationships because we think we are powerless to change them. Many of us then resign ourselves to endure problem marriages, parent-child difficulties, work hassles, and loneliness. Or we see situations as hopeless and remove ourselves from them. In this way we create a lot of our own unhappiness.

From the steps listed above, you will be able to move into all aspects of your life and apply what you have learned. At first, you may just look at improving things where you work. Then you can begin to explore your friendships. Finally, you might take a look at your close relationships. The formula is equally suitable for building your career or for improving your marriage. The goal is to increase your skill in improving interpersonal relationships.

You will find that these skills apply not just in your personal life, but that many will be helpful in work team relationships. Understanding the way people relate to each other will make you more aware of communication styles of co-workers and potential employers. This will help you to understand what is required of you to be successful in your job.

STEP 5: IMPLEMENT YOUR PERSONAL LIFE MANAGEMENT PLAN

Implement your **Personal Life Management Plan** wherever you feel the need. You are, indeed, in charge of your future and your happiness: not fate, not your friends, not your boss. Improving the way you relate to other people, and developing a sound sense of what you need to improve in all aspects of your life, will take you ever closer to lasting serenity, to a life without struggle and desperation. It will become your personal road map for high performance.

With this formula you yourself will build a new, more workable and satisfying lifestyle pattern. Remember, at each step you alter your potential; you improve your ability to succeed in your own life choices.

The formula is complete:

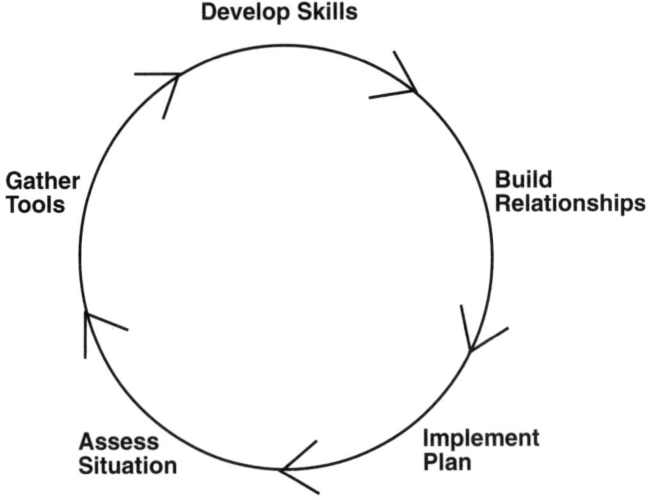

This gives you *new potential* for a *new destiny.*

Any person's destiny is the end product of what that individual believes can happen and then lives or acts out.

The course of history has been changed recently by a man who believed communism couldn't work anymore and who let that belief drive all his actions. The resulting opening up of the former Soviet Union to the rest of the world began with one person who chose to think and live a different destiny. He increased the potential for successful change for an entire nation.

On the other hand, there are those who create a negative destiny. Someone who is addicted to drugs and/or alcohol may cry that he or she is powerless to be anything but an addict, so that person will live life that way. Only those that see addiction as a lifestyle that has grown out of a set of choices can truly recover their sense of direction and control.

You've probably heard people say they are "born" to a certain destiny, while others "seek" their destiny. Right here, right now, I am suggesting to you that it is your road, your life. If you like it, congratulations! You have found the key to lasting happiness. But if you don't, **you can begin to think in terms of defining your own potential through managing your life.**

The idea that is paramount in this book is:

You can change your potential and your destiny by developing a clear *Personal Life Management Plan.*

The unfortunate condition of adulthood is the acceptance of what we call "reality". For so many, reality is the world of what "can't happen." This world is dismal in its lack of potential for change and happiness. Very young children do not see the world this way. They see it as full of promise and delight. Every event is an adventure; every spring a wonder.

But, somewhere along the way children "get smart." They learn the disappointment of the fantasy that doesn't come true. After many disappointments they learn not to set their sights too high, so their chance for happiness becomes limited by their view of a limited potential. Then, in their minds—in our minds— the world becomes not okay; it is a place of unfulfilled expectations.

The "logical" conclusion for us as adults becomes, then, that dreaming is a foolish waste of time. But without the dream of what can be, we have no road map for the journey to our own happiness. We then give the power over our future away to some unguided "fate" that buffets us about with the changing circumstances of the day.

Your dreams are the doorway to your potential. Change, skills, life management are all in your control and are all ways you can have the future you desire. In the activity below you will be asked to put away the negative "reality" you have spent most of your life learning and to dream. Your dreams are important.

PERSONAL LIFE MANAGEMENT SKILL #1
DEFINE YOUR DREAM

At this point, you should pause and pull together your thoughts on the formula. Defining your expectation in life, or for the use of this book, is an important first step.

Write, in as much detail as possible, your dream for a successful life. Define it clearly. Don't worry now if it appears realistic or not. It's your dream, be free with it.

1. My dream for my friendships is:

2. My dream for my family is:

3. My dream for my love relationships is:

4. My dream for my career is:

PERSONAL LIFE MANAGEMENT PLAN STEP #1

Define Your Dream

2 Realizing Your Potential through Change

What most of us really want is to have a life that brings us minimal hardship, satisfying relationships, and reasonable security. Maybe your life was working great a year ago, or last month, or before you started this new relationship, or before you lost your old job. But now there are parts that just aren't coming together for you. Some people feel this as a restlessness or a general sadness. You may experience it as a dissatisfaction that seems to have no specific cause. As you look at what your circumstances are, and at who you are today, you may find you'd like to change some things to bring your life around.

"I know that. That's why I'm reading this book," you say. Good first step. But are you ready to accept change—not change in people and circumstances around you—change in you and change in the way you approach all aspects of your life? That's not quite as easy as just reading a book, is it? In fact, so many people become overwhelmed with just how big a job changing might be, that they do nothing at all.

Sadly, fear of change often paralyzes us and prevents our taking the first step to make our lives work better. This is nothing new, either. History and literature are full of failed leaders who wouldn't change. Certainly, everyday people have the same problem. The experience of Ben, a production worker in a textile plant, is a good illustration.

Ben came to me as a referral from his company counselor. He had enough seniority for a promotion, but the other workers found him difficult to deal with and just plain didn't like him. When I asked Ben what he thought his problem was, he responded, "They don't respect me. I am who I am, and they can take me or leave me. I don't care." This kind of attitude is often a defense for the sadness created by rejection. Ben desperately wanted the promotion and genuinely wanted to be liked by the other workers, but he had no idea what to do to make that happen.

We talked about change. He resisted the idea strongly, "They are the problem. Why should I have to change?" In counseling, he thought he was going to learn how to "straighten out" the other employees. What Ben eventually understood, however, was that he was partly responsible for how people reacted to him. He also realized that the only way things would go better at the plant was for him to modify the way he related to the other workers.

It has taken time, but Ben is making change work for him—he looks at others' reactions to what he says and how he acts. Then, he comes up with ways to communicate more effectively. He has been very successful in creating a plan for continued improvement. Things are going better at work, and each week he reports some new incident that supports his new "attitude."

Ben, like so many of us, was afraid to do anything different, even though his personal behavior pattern wasn't working for him. He found, though, that he could have an effect on what was happening to him; he could even make choices about how he came across to others. He made change work for him—just like you can.

In the activity below you will write down changes you would like to see in your own life. Perhaps you like many things about your life the way they are, and there are just one or two areas you would prefer to be different. Or, you may be one of those people who is just fed up with everything and wish to "start over." Either way, writing down the changes you need or want is the first step.

Assessment Activity # 1

List four changes you would like to see take place in your life.

1.

2.

3.

4.

(Note: Just the act of writing down the most important areas of needed change will help you to focus energy toward making those changes happen.)

You have identified the areas you would like to see change. As you look back over the list, you might notice that there are some items on it that you just wish would be different. An example might be, "I wish I were living in a different part of the country." Other people might wish for a different appearance or a nicer house or a vacation to a tropical island. Looking now at the change items you listed, choose which ones are the "wouldn't it be nice if this happened to me" kinds of changes. Then, look for the "I am willing to expend time and effort to make these happen" kinds of changes.

From a personal development view, the changes for which you are willing to work are obviously the best place to spend your effort. But the wishful kinds of changes can oftentimes motivate you toward goal setting and meaningful work. Both kinds are important to consider.

DEALING WITH CHANGE

Change occurs in our lives in two ways. Some change just happens. Other change is of our doing. Let's take a look at what change really means and how we can work with it as a contribution to personal growth.

There are two types of change to consider :

1. Changes that happen to you.
2. Changes that you create yourself.

CHANGES THAT HAPPEN TO YOU

These include such things as: winning the lottery, finding a rare painting, having children, earthquakes, airplanes falling on you while you are on the interstate, random shootings on the street or in the mall, unexpected layoffs or moves, and having a dog or cat move in with your family. All of these are uninitiated by you. Some have pleasant results; others have not-so-pleasant results.

Assessment Activity #2

List below several changes that affected you directly over the last year that were unexpected and out of your control. Then, write how you reacted to those changes when they occurred.

1. Change #1:

   Reaction:

2. Change #2:

   Reaction:

3. Change #3:

   Reaction:

In this first kind of change you have little or no warning or control to stop the event from occurring. You may, though, be able to prepare for or alter the effect of the occurrence in some way. For instance, you can keep a current resume and maintain contacts in your field in preparation for unexpected layoffs, take a defensive driving course, or practice "street sense" techniques in a safety/self-defense class.

Change can inspire fear because of the sheer unexpectedness of the events. Those who fare best under unexpected circumstances are those who accept that a certain number of these kinds of life upheavals will just happen. And further, they refuse to live in fear of them. Staying away from malls to avoid being shot by a crazed sniper is unrealistic. However, cultivating a heightened awareness of how to respond in emergency situations could help you to come successfully out of even the worst scenarios, personal or professional. The **key is to not hand over control of your life and not allow yourself to be the victim of fate, but instead, to become motivated to deal with the change in a positive way.**

REACTING TO CHANGES THAT HAPPEN TO YOU

A lot of how change affects you depends on your attitude toward it. Changes are opportunities for some, tragedies for others. Scott and Linda are a prime example. Scott, a marketing manager for a consumer products firm, found out his company was being sold and he would be laid off. He went into an immediate depression. His wife, Linda, a city planner, began to figure out how their schedules, budget, and lifestyle could work around the new situation.

Said Scott, "My career will be set back five years. I don't know what to do now. Where will I work? How can we have a life with so much uncertainty?" Said Linda, "There will be difficulties, I am sure, but I look forward to helping Scott look at his options. We might even be able to afford for him not to work for a year, so he can make a career change. In some ways I almost envy him."

Scott had a past history with many life-rending changes that had, for the most part, gone badly for him. Linda's upbringing gave her a different perspective. For her, change was a sort of adventure, "to see what you can make of it."

What Do You Think?

Adam is a professional athlete with a college degree. He understands that at his age he has about four years left to participate in his sport. Brainstorm to suggest conditions that will affect Adam's choices as he approaches retirement. What might some positive outcomes of a career change be for Adam?

Your view of change as a curse or an opportunity is indeed in your control. You may say that you can't control the power going out in your house during a storm. This is true. But you can be prepared for such an event, or you can find creative ways to stay cool, or warm, or to be entertained during the outage.

We don't have to be expecting and prepared for all changes in our lives for them to turn out to be good for us. A move or a change in job may be unsettling at first but, after time, may be just the boost you needed to get things going.

As change becomes more and more a part of our daily lives, fear of it becomes not only useless, but can actually be detrimental if it paralyzes us. Fear can stimulate you to outrun an assailant, or it can freeze you into powerlessness and inability to move forward, to respond. The same energy that comes from fear can be used to power positive responses. **We can allow ourselves to be motivated by change if we develop good tactics for dealing with it.**

STRATEGIES FOR MANAGING CHANGE THAT HAPPENS TO YOU

Since change is probably going to be more common in our lives than non-change, we have to learn to develop strategies to manage change. For change that happens to us we can take three paths to make the experience positive. Those paths are: **resilience, perception, and expectation.**

The first step, then, in managing change is to **cultivate resilience.** By becoming less agitated and more adaptable in the face of change, we reduce our stress level. New challenges and conditions will greet us each day of our lives. Granted, some will be more profound than others. But, if a company stops making your favorite cereal, you are better off finding a new cereal than in getting upset over the action. In the same vein, if you are asked to do your job on new equipment or with new procedures, you will be much calmer if you approach it as a learning challenge, not a threat.

Assessment Activity #3

Look at your responses in Activity #2. Is there anything you could do now to alter the effects of the changes you listed?

Example: Work has slowed and two of my closest friends have been laid off.This change makes me feel afraid for my own job and worried about my friends.

Resilient response: I can feel good about the fact that my company values me enough to keep me, and I am learning new things in my expanded job role.

For my friends, I can help them by giving them contacts for new jobs and maybe just taking them to lunch for moral support.

For myself, I will update my resume and continue attending club and professional meetings to keep my contacts up to date.

1. Change event:

   Resilient response plan:

2. Change event:

   Resilient response plan:

3. Change event:

   Resilient response plan:

The second step in managing change is to **increase perception. You are less likely to be taken by surprise by events in your work or life if you are aware of what is going on in the world.** If you lived in Louisiana in the early eighties and were dependent on the gas industry for your job, you either realized a crisis was coming and sought work elsewhere, or you were taken by surprise when your company closed.

If you understand what factors in the world affect you personally, you will see trends and positive directions you can follow. With pollution growing in our major cities, it is only a matter of time until we will have to exchange our gasoline-powered automobiles for electric or other alternative transportation. Realizing this, the car manufacturers are doing early research on electric vehicles. They want to be informed about changing conditions. By being informed, you too can plan changes in your life that will help you adapt to new conditions as they evolve.

Assessment Activity #4

Take a moment and think about the kinds of outside events or conditions that could affect your life in some way.

1. Outside events that could directly or indirectly affect my life:

   What effect could these events have on my life if they occur?

What can I do to make these events support my efforts to improve my life?

2. Outside events that could affect my work or education:

   What effect could these events have if they occur?

   What can I do to make these events support my efforts to improve my life?

The third area of effective response to change is meeting it with a **positive expectation.** As in the case of Linda and Scott above, Linda's expectation of a positive outcome led her to some good problem solving and clear weighing of alternatives. Scott's negative expectation led him to worry and despair. Of course not all changes will benefit you immediately, but many can work out to your advantage in the long run.

Beginning with an expectation that changes will ultimately be good for you is an important first step. It is difficult, indeed, to feel positive or powerful if your view of new events or conditions is gloomy. If nothing else, **positive expectation makes us feel hopeful, and out of this hopefulness comes clear thinking that can lead the event to a positive outcome.**

Assessment Activity #5

Refer to the list you did in Activity #2. What were some positive outcomes of the changes?

1.

2.

3.

Were there any negative outcomes?

If so, what were they?

Could your reaction have affected the outcome positively or negatively? How?

CHANGES YOU CREATE YOURSELF

Change will come. It will not always be at a time that is good for you. It may not always be a change that you will prefer. In order to continue to prosper and grow in your life, you can't just tread water in the flood of new events. Sometimes you have to jump into that flood and learn to surf, or get a boat, or maybe build a dam and generate electricity.

The key to managing change is to **live forward. What is past cannot be viewed as either a monument or a curse. It must, instead, be a springboard, a launch site.** Time and events go forward. People who do not also go forward run the risk of being weighed down by the old events and bewildered by new circumstances. Your life will be different every day. You can choose positively: to grow, to learn, to move with change, to become more understanding about events, to develop new life and professional skills, to cultivate new relationships and improve old ones. Or you can choose not to.

By definition, life management, self-development, and effective living suggest a strategy of change, of dynamic movement, of adaptation, and of growth. By taking change as a way to become more skilled at dealing with the world, and the people and events in it, you choose to grow in the direction that will create the most happiness for you. **Choose change; create your own destiny.**

There are few people who change because they simply decide they need a new challenge. Most seek change to eliminate some discomfort in their lives. Crisis and pain often cause quick and radical changes in people. If we view discomfort as a motivator, a reason to change to a new, more effective behavior, then it could become a welcome signal.

Perhaps that is the place to start.

PERSONAL LIFE MANAGEMENT SKILL #1
FIND AREAS OF DISCOMFORT

Try to isolate the areas in your life today that are making you uncomfortable or maybe are causing a crisis for you. List them below. (Remember, list *only* those things that are creating a problem for you, not something someone else would like you to alter.)

1. Area #1:

2. Area #2:

3. Area #3:

The number here is limited to three because generally only two or three areas cause you enough discomfort to consider change. As you begin this change process and become comfortable with it, you can certainly address additional areas. Now for each of these areas, list what the rewards of change will be for you.

Area #1: Rewards of change:

Area #2: Rewards of change:

Area #3: Rewards of change:

QUICK TIPS TO MAKE CHANGE EASY

After you have made a decision as to what to change about yourself and/or your life, you can use these tips that follow to aid the process. Before you begin, though, make sure that you have clearly decided upon what you want to change.

The first step is to **make a commitment.** In order to make your change plans materialize, you will have to commit to follow-through on the work that will be involved in making the change. This commitment is the determination to be persistent, no matter how inconvenient or difficult the task may become. Without commitment there is often halfhearted effort leading to only partial success. Commitment is the driving force that will steer you in the direction you need. It will assure you of the desired reward you seek.

PERSONAL LIFE MANAGEMENT SKILL #2
MAKE A COMMITMENT

Choose two of the items that you listed in Step #1 that you would like to change.

Write your commitment statement for each below:

1. Desired change #1:

   I commit to:

2. Desired change #2:

   I commit to:

After commitment comes **visualization.** This is a technique that many successful individuals practice. There are several steps to this process, but once you practice them a few times, you will find them to be automatic.

PERSONAL LIFE MANAGEMENT SKILL #3
VISUALIZE CHANGE

1. In a quiet place relax your body and clear your mind of all thoughts.
2. Create a picture in your mind of the desired change as if it now exists. Remember to put in as much detail as you can.
3. Put yourself in the scene and actually picture yourself working toward the new conditions that will bring happiness.

Now that you have done this, write down in as much detail as possible your vision of what the change will look like and be like. You can do this for each of the changes you have selected, but it is best to concentrate on one at a time.

My change vision looked like:

The more detail you can bring into these scenes, the clearer your path to change will be. You will know exactly what you will have to do to arrive at the change you seek. What is important is not the scene itself but the practicing of this technique over and over. Each time you do it, the scene and the activities required to reach your goal will become clearer. In addition, you will find that your sense of purpose and determination increases with each practice.

The only caution in this is that you focus on changes for you only. Attempts to create change in your life by wanting others to change or by wishing harm to others is ineffective and can be unhealthy. Your unconscious can be very powerful, so be certain that you are committed to a positive outcome. You may get everything you ask for.

After you get a clear picture of the new conditions you are moving toward, decide what behaviors you will need to bring you to that point. You may need new skills; you may need to do some familiar things differently. In practice, these new behaviors may feel awkward at first, but don't worry about that. Remember your commitment to follow-through and be persistent. Allow yourself several weeks to get used to the new ways of doing things. Changes do not happen in 24-hour time blocks.

The next step is to **practice** the actions or thoughts that are required to get you to your desired outcome. This part is so important to your success. Making the special effort required will let you feel good every day. But if you backslide and miss occasionally, don't worry about it. Give yourself permission to be imperfect occasionally, then get back to your goal activities right away.

An important hint here is that practicing in your mind is often as beneficial as practicing an action. One skill you will learn in this book in a later chapter is how to manage conflict situations. You will be able to practice the skills related to managing these by rehearsing example conflict scenes in your mind and applying your new knowledge toward solving them. No one will see you do this, and you will be better prepared when real situations occur.

PERSONAL LIFE MANAGEMENT SKILL #4
PRACTICE CHANGE BEHAVIORS

From your visualization activity, write down three or four behaviors or thought patterns you need to practice. Then, write down ways you could practice these in your daily life.

1. Practice area #1:

   Practice plan:

2. Practice area #2:

   Practice plan:

3. Practice area #3:

   Practice plan:

The final tip is the same one we started with—**relax.** Let yourself go through the change process in a calm way. Don't hassle yourself. Be prepared for unexpected occurrences. And above all, don't panic if the desired change does not occur immediately. These things happen in their own time—when you are ready—not when you think you are ready. Trust your subconscious to guide you in the direction you have set.

You can be a change agent for yourself. **Life can be a creative process of directing your energy, anticipating changes in the world around you, and designing positive outcomes.** In the chapters that follow, you will learn step-by-step skills to make the process go better for you. These skills will give you a firm footing in the change journey and help you enjoy regular successes along the way.

As you answer the thought-provoking questions in each chapter, you may even choose to re-focus your original change plan. You will be learning skills that will give you more general knowledge and specific "how-to's" in many areas. So, you may want to expand your vision of a satisfying destiny. You will receive support and assistance at every step.

Live forward. Choose change.

PERSONAL LIFE MANAGEMENT PLAN STEP #2

Find Areas of Discomfort

Make a Commitment

Visualize the Change

Practice Change Behaviors

UNIT I
PROGRESS CHECK AND AFFIRMATION

Dear Reader:

In chapters 1 and 2 you have taken some very important first steps:

1. You have dared to dream and believe the value of the dream.
2. You have realized the need for change and accepted the role of personal change agent for yourself.

The **Personal Life Management Plan** that you have begun grows out of the model introduced to you in Chapter 1. By committing to a dream and devising a plan to realize that dream, you light the path to positive self-growth. In the following two chapters you will be learning some new skills that will become your tools for crafting a life of your very own design.

Up to now we have only asked you to accept the idea of change as it relates to achieving your goals. As you progress through this book, you will begin applying the skills that you learn on a daily basis. Our part in this is to make each step a careful and well-designed contribution to your progress. Your part is to persevere in reading and practicing what you learn.

You are the designer of your **Personal Life Management Plan.** You use it however you feel is best for your situation. But be assured that many have gone before you and have experienced increased control and purpose in their lives.

We will be with you throughout this entire process and intend to support you 100 percent.

You can do this! You can do it well!

Sincerely,
B.W. and S. Mc.

STAGE TWO: GATHER NECESSARY TOOLS

Organizing Time and Tasks

John's office is neat in the morning when he arrives, in the evening when he leaves, and even during the day while he is working. Sherry works, drives in a car pool, and is the team mother for the little league team. Both of these people appear organized and in control of their lives. They are also living examples to the rest of us who wish we could be that way.

Though some people are more structured and detailed than others, most of us agree we could improve in this area. The difficulty is that you, like everyone else, have "multiple priorities" in your life, that is, many important things to accomplish and rarely enough time to do them. Whether you are an executive who directs a multi-million dollar company, an electrician who wires whole buildings, or an at-home mother who balances parenting with running a household, you know how necessary being organized is.

Granted, there are some (I'm sure you know a few) who seem to be born to be orderly. A few are trained to be that way, as in the military. Some of us, though, never seem to quite get that part of our lives under control—try as we might. But having a life where you can plan, get things done, and still find time for yourself and for those you care about *is* possible.

The case of Ellen and her husband Ahmed is an example. Ellen is a professional musician and travels a great deal. Ahmed is an accountant with a large company and also works long hours. They came to me for marriage counseling because, as they put it, "We don't have time to be married anymore." It seemed that when Ahmed had a day off, or could take one, Ellen was out of town. When Ellen came in from a trip and wanted to spend time with Ahmed, he had to work late to meet a deadline.

"We used to just enjoy being together: discovering out-of-the-way restaurants, listening to unknown bands playing in neighborhood bars, or even just feeding the ducks in the city lake. Now, we don't have time for anything."

In the activity below you will be asked to make a start on the road to organization by choosing those parts of your life you wish to handle better.

Assessment Activity #1

I wish I had more time for

____

____.

I believe that if I managed ________________________ better, my life would seem more organized.

Now, you have begun the process of uncovering the problem areas. You may have had the same experience as Ellen and Ahmed; you are caught up in demands on your time. Yet, you do not command your time. Fortunately, making choices for change worked for them, and it will for you.

This chapter is about how to manage your life's daily demands. It is not like those books that casually dismiss the problem by saying, "Don't sweat the small stuff." If your life is like mine, you wish there was some "small stuff." It **all** seems like "big stuff." That is why it is difficult to manage. Understanding how you look at organization in general will help you see why some situations are more difficult for you to "get a handle on" than others. In addition, in this chapter you will develop the skills you need to approach life's time and task challenges in a confident and successful way.

WHY WE HAVE TROUBLE WITH ORGANIZATION

People who seem like "born organizers" in some respects really are. Just by the way their brain works, some people think and operate naturally in a methodical, structured manner. These people are probably not reading this chapter, so don't worry about feeling intimidated by them anymore. You are going to learn to do the same thing with your life, and no one will ever know you weren't a "born organizer" yourself.

First, we will explore the difficulty most of us have in gaining a sense of control. There are many reasons for this difficulty, and they range from everyone's demands on us, to our own inability to manage too many and diverse tasks. Most of these reasons, however, stem from the same sources: our thinking styles, our lack of skill training, and our inability to say "no." All of which can make us ill-equipped for the complexity of adult life.

THINKING STYLES

The way thinking style enters into our ability to manage our time and tasks is best shown by the example of two brothers: Kyle, nine, and George, six. Both have the task of cleaning their rooms, which are perfect examples of chaos and disarray. Kyle looks at the mess and sees the room as a gigantic, insurmountable mountain of disorder. Being completely overwhelmed by the immenseness of the task, he becomes agitated, tries picking up a few pieces, then begins to wander around aimlessly. Eventually, he says he cannot do it alone and begs for help.

George, on the other hand, surveys the mess (equally intimidating looking to the observer) and attacks parts of the task separately: toys, then clothes, then bed, then sweeping. He is done in half an hour. There are a few pieces that did not quite make it to the proper places, but on the whole, the task of making the room look better was accomplished.

On the adult level we see this in another way. Angus, a mechanic, listens to a car's sounds, feels like he knows what the problem is, and goes to it. If he is incorrect about his guess, he listens again and tries again. His partner, Aaron, approaches car repair differently. When a car comes in, he goes through a series of diagnostic procedures to isolate the problem. Both are successful mechanics with high customer satisfaction.

Angus makes slightly more errors than Aaron on the first try, but he corrects them quickly and is often finished with his cars for the day before Aaron. Aaron regularly takes longer than Angus, but seldom makes an error. When he does, he usually calls Angus in because the problem is generally some new or perplexing difficulty he doesn't have a procedure for uncovering.

Who is more "organized"? Aaron appears to be, but Angus likely has a clear process he uses that isn't apparent to the observer. Angus is a gifted, intuitive, gut-level car mechanic. But sometimes his first impulse is wrong. Aaron is a methodical, perseverant, well-trained problem solver. Sometimes, though, the problem is outside the expected, and he can't discover the solution. The success of their business is that the combination of the two styles can handle anything that comes along.

You probably have ways you approach organizing or performing tasks that work quite well. But though successful in some situations, in others these methods don't work at all. A typical complaint by my own clients is, "You know I am incredibly well-organized at work, but at home I just can't seem to get it together."

By understanding your approach to organization, you will quickly see why some tasks overwhelm and paralyze you and others don't. As soon as you have a clear picture of your style, you will be able to learn additional approaches to apply to other, "monster level" challenges.

Assessment Activity #2

Write below situations where you have handled a challenging project well. List two or three with as much detail as you can.

Challenge #1:

What I did to make it turn out well:

Challenge #2:

What I did to make it turn out well:

Challenge #3:

What I did to make it turn out well:

Now, look at the types of challenges each of these represents, and at your approach to the challenge. Identify your task management style as "quick, creative thinking" or "careful, methodical thinking."

My style is (choose one of the above and write it here):

Let's be careful here not to confuse a natural organizational style with the conclusions conveyed in the following: "I guess I'm just born to be messy. I know my mother was, so I guess I inherited it." There is not, to the knowledge of medical science, a "you will be disorganized" gene. You can draw a valid conclusion, though, that your approach to organization may predispose you to have difficulty with certain situations. This is why you will need to learn skills to help you with those challenges you cannot solve easily.

By knowing your natural approach to managing complex or difficult demands on your time and energies, you can begin to develop skills in the other methods for handling these. Skill development is important because few of us have received the training along the way to prepare us for the diverse demands our adult lives produce.

SKILLS DEVELOPMENT

When we are young, life is relatively simple compared to when we are grown. One reason is that when we are young we don't have as many "things," in the way of personal property to keep track of or maintain. Car ownership, for example, brings with it car payments, insurance payments, oil changes, tire rotation, exterior washing, etc. None of this exists for the young person. So, as young people, we rarely develop good organizational or planning skills.

Another difference from youth to adulthood is the increase in number and complexity of the many roles we are expected to play, such as: working person, single person, married person, parent, caretaker of parents, co-worker, boss, meal planner, house cleaner, bill payer, friend, confidant, and on and on. The most visible evidence of this difference is mail.

A child receives cards at birthday and Christmas, an occasional letter from Grandma, a coupon for a cereal or toy, and maybe a magazine from Aunt Genie. That's pretty much it. Adults, on the other hand, have to allot time just to sort through the mail that consists of bills, letters, catalogs, ads, coupons, contests, and tons of other miscellaneous mail pieces. In addition to mail, adults are subjected to barrages of phone sales calls for everything from the daily newspaper to resort time shares.

When you were a child, you managed your school life and your own social life with help from Mom and Dad and maybe a brother or sister. When you become an adult, you manage your own life plus you must assist those with whom you interact. You counsel a friend, coach an employee, help your boss, haul the kids, meet a co-worker for lunch, call your aging parent, or visit your sister .

Whew! How do you do it? Most of us feel like we end up not handling any of what we do well. Some of your success at managing your tasks depends on the skills you have been taught.

In the assessment activity below you will report any skill training from your childhood or adult life experience that has taught you to handle multiple tasks.

Assessment Activity #3

In this activity you will write down organizational activities you were taught while growing up. For example, "My father taught me that paying bills as they come in helps to prevent a pile up at due dates." Some are not so helpful. "I remember my brother always piled his clothes in the corner and used to yell when he didn't have anything clean to wear out on a date. I don't ever recall seeing him plan what he would wear on the weekend and then getting it washed."

Skill training example #1— I remember:

Skill training example #2— I remember:

Skill training example #3— I remember:

If you are like most, unless you have attended seminars, read books, or received specific instruction on methods for managing multiple tasks, you probably do not have a good set of skills to apply. But even the most skilled person cannot utilize that training until he or she learns to be assertive about the need to organize.

SAYING "NO"

Too often our lives become overloaded not by those tasks required to maintain ourselves at home and at work, but by those tasks "required" by others. I put required in quotes here because that is the way the situation appears, but in reality, may not be.

There is no intention to be sexist here, but women seem to fall into this pattern more often than men. Men can, though, be just as easily drawn into "requirements" of others, especially at work.

Is this a picture of your life?

Stephanie is the shift leader and the union representative at the auto manufacturing plant. She is also a deacon at her church and mother of three children, two of them teenagers. "Stephanie, can you stay late today? Some senior managers are coming in and want to meet with you on that new benefits proposal." "Stephanie, we need someone with your experience to manage the fund-raiser for the new fellowship hall." "Mom, would you drive Zack and me to the ballgame and pick us up at Benny's at nine? Oh, and can you change my orthodontist's appointment to next week? A wire broke on my braces."

Mack is an engineer with a software applications company. He is heading out the door at the end of the day in order to attend a professional meeting.

A co-worker calls to him, "Mack, the Jackson account software has bugs in it, and they're expecting installation on Thursday. Can you help me with it? We really have to meet that deadline or we lose credibility with the customer."

In both of these cases, the individuals involved felt fully entitled to make requests of Stephanie's and Mack's time—they needed it. In both these cases a "No, I'm sorry, I have another obligation" in response to requests might have kept them from feeling overloaded. A six-year-old can make his own sandwich, but he prefers to have Mom do it. A co-worker can handle his or her own job, but prefers to have help. Other people's priorities can become yours very quickly if you let them.

Have you fallen into this pattern with those you live and work with?

Assessment Activity #4

Write below three things that have been asked of you this week which you really didn't have time or energy for, but you did anyway.

Request #1:

Request #2:

Request #3:

Now, could the person who requested any of these perform the task without your help? (Be honest on this one. Being needed is nice, but being stretched beyond your own limits when it is not necessary is stressful.)

Like any other challenge, though, **this time and task management issue is addressed at two levels: defining the challenge and developing skills to meet it.** In the activity above you have begun by defining the challenges. For the skills, we can draw from the experience of professionals who manage complex tasks and deadlines for a living. These people are called project managers, and they have some helpful approaches we can use in our own daily lives. They accomplish their goals by keeping three issues in focus regardless of the size or complexity of the job:

Setting priorities
Locating and using resources
Completing tasks

You can move one step closer to being a successful "life manager" by learning what these professionals know and utilize everyday. In the **Personal Life Management Plan** steps that follow, you will be guided in methods for organizing your own time and tasks.

SETTING PRIORITIES

Figuring out the most important and productive ways to spend your time has probably been a difficulty for you. Everyone has limited time; most of us work hard. Yet, some people accomplish a lot, while others just get tired. How is it that with the same number of hours in a day some get more done than others? Successful organizers plan. They take the time to think about a job or goal activity to decide what is most important to finish. Then, they direct their time and energy there. They understand the notion of the **necessary track.** (Note: In the business management field of project management this is called the "critical path.")

The **necessary track** is the set of steps you have to go through, in proper order, to fulfill your goal. For example, if the goal is to get to work on time, specific activities must be completed in order:

Morning Routine

1. Get up at 6 A.M.
2. Shower
3. Dress *Make coffee
4. Eat breakfast
5. Feed dog
6. Set burglar alarm
7. Lock door

Some things may be done simultaneously (*). You can have coffee brewing and toast browning while you dress, for instance. But there are always parts of the process that must occur in order, and you will have to complete all the necessary track steps to reach your goal satisfactorily.

This is why some people generate a lot of activity on their jobs, and always look busy but never get anything significant done. They have not figured out what the necessary tracks of their tasks are. So, they are not likely to complete anything. We must get a picture of what the necessary track steps are and pursue them in order: *Prioritize.*

Chris wants to build a fence for the dog. He knows that he will have to have his property surveyed, to buy what he needs, and to put the fence up. He can't buy materials until he has the survey so that he can measure to see how much he needs. He can't put up the fence until he has all the materials. Another important element to this picture is that if Chris does not prioritize fencebuilding in terms of specific steps and allow time for each one in order, he will not reach his goal.

The necessary track helps to set priorities. Prioritizing helps him to plan the best use of his time in other ways. If he has two hours to wait for a plane or an hour at the doctor's office, his priorities will lead him to make up his list of materials or draw his fence plan, instead of sitting in the airport bar or reading a magazine at the doctor's office.

Linda needs to upgrade her work skills to get a raise. Her goal is the raise. The necessary track includes a class two nights a week for six weeks. Her priorities say that some of her evening activities will have to be replaced by class work. Any activity that is not on the necessary track is considered a lower priority.

Remember, stress can occur in your life when you don't do what you think you really should be doing. Sometimes if you get distracted, the necessary track will remind you to keep focused. Being happy with yourself for completing each step toward your goal is easier when the steps are clearly defined and priorities are set for their completion. **If someone tries to involve you in an activity that is not on your necessary track, then you should decline.**

Two hints will help you here: make sure phone calls meet your needs and not someone else's. Our adolescence left us with a priority on answering the phone because of the teenager's need to communicate. As adults, we have to separate that urge from a real communication need that supports our goals. In other words, use a machine or let the phone ring during the times you are working on your necessary track items. Sales calls and chatty friends have a high need to communicate with you. This may not support your need to complete your necessary track steps.

The other hint is to **throw away all that junk mail without opening it.** The time it takes to wade through all the worthless "stuff" could be spent meeting your own goals. Time is allotted to each of us in the same way each day. How we use that time is sometimes the difference between accomplishment and frustration. By eliminating some activities, at least for the time you are pursuing a specific goal, you make yourself available for your necessary track items.

Speaking of time, each one of your necessary track steps takes time. Carefully assessing the time required to perform each step will help you plan more successfully. In the **Personal Life Management Plan** step below you will be building your path toward your goals by listing the necessary track items, in order, and estimating the time you will have to allow for their completion.

PERSONAL LIFE MANAGEMENT SKILL #1
PRIORITIZE NECESSARY TRACK

Choose one goal you want to accomplish in the next two weeks. Develop the necessary track steps and decide the order in which they must be done. Also, estimate the time needed to complete each one.

Goal: Deadline for completion:

Necessary Track Time needed

Step 1:

Step 2:

Step 3:

Step 4:

Now you have drawn a clear picture of the tasks required to reach your goal. In the action step above, you have written down goals, steps, and time required. You will be able to make a realistic plan toward making those steps happen. The next part of the process is to determine what equipment, supplies, or help you will need.

SECURING NECESSARY RESOURCES

You have probably driven down the road behind an old pickup truck that is loaded with pine straw, bags of grass seed, small shrubs, and an assortment of shovels, rakes, and brooms. In addition, there may even be a lawn mower balanced tentatively on top of it all. This truck is an example of good resource planning. Lawn care businesses send out their workers in the morning loaded for the day's work. A trip back to the storage site to pick up some supplies or tools would be time-consuming and unprofitable. Planning, based on the jobs of the day, prevents extra trips or unnecessary purchases.

At a technology research lab, failure to have the needed electronic parts on hand can delay development and delivery of a half-million-dollar product to a customer. In your own life you have probably been frustrated more than once when the pen by the phone is out of ink or there is no paper to take a note on. This is a simple problem, but having resources needed to perform a task is necessary to make your life flow smoothly.

Gathering resources for any task requires that you must think about what you need to achieve what you want to do. Back to the example of Chris, who was building a fence, we observe a good resource planner. Having never built a fence before, he went to a building supply store and bought a book that made several suggestions. He learned that crushed gravel in the fence post holes worked better than cement and was easier to use. In addition, he found out that he had to have a recent survey of his property, so his fence wouldn't end up on his neighbor's land.

The booklet also suggested the types of fence pullers and other tools he would need. So with about two hours' planning, Chris saved himself nearly a day's time because he wouldn't have to stop to get something he needed. He also saved himself the irritation of needing something he did not have. In an interesting aside, Chris learned the first day that he was lacking another important resource—help. As you do your planning, don't forget to include the human resource factor—people to help you do what needs to be done.

Most adults have many tasks to accomplish in their everyday lives. Some are as simple as the daily routine of getting out the door to work or school (not so simple when there are children involved, as any parent will attest). Others, though, are more complicated, like buying a car or trying to change jobs. Resource planning is an important "think through" process you will find to be a great help.

Remember that you might not be a "think through" person by nature. If you are not, then you probably have quite a few tasks that frustrate you because you cannot seem to get them out of the way. Below, you will find a **Personal Life Management Plan** step to help you complete your goal activity. The guidelines offered in this step will help you to be organized in your resource planning.

PERSONAL LIFE MANAGEMENT PLAN STEP #2
SECURING RESOURCES

Looking back to the goals you have set for projects or tasks, choose one you would like to complete in the next two weeks. List below what resources you will need to make the job go well.

Goal:

Resources list:

Supplies:

Tools/equipment:

Human resources:

(Note: For each one of these it is also helpful to write down where you will find it. Tools can be rented; human resource skills can be hired or traded for favors with friends or neighbors. Thinking this out before you begin your task will help completion go faster.)

Resources I need to buy:	How much?	Where?

Resources I can make or rent:	How much?	Where?

People I know who can help:	Hire?	Friend/favor?

Resource planning, like any other planning, takes time. This is why so many people don't plan. They get into a frenzy of "I have to get started." What they don't realize, though, is that people who don't plan frequently spend a great deal more time on their tasks than those who do plan—including planning time. At the end of this chapter is a planning sheet built from the guidlines in the **Personal Life Management Plan** steps. Make copies and use them whenever you have a project to complete.

What Do You Think?

Howard needs to prepare two proposals for clients of his company by Friday. His children have a baseball game on Thursday night, and he has promised to attend. Howard's goal is to accomplish both by the end of the week without sacrificing one or the other.

What are the necessary track items for Howard's task?

What resources would you suggest Howard use in completing the tasks?

COMPLETING TASKS

The final step in organizing is completing tasks. This seems like a natural result of attempting a task, but many things can interfere with our efforts. We will look at a few common interferences and help you develop strategies to deal with them.

They are:

1. Time just gets away.
2. There are too many things to do to finish any.

How many days have we started the morning with great intentions? I myself have even taken a day of leave from work just to "catch up." For the barriers listed above to completing a task or reaching a goal, the solution is **awareness.**

TIME JUST GETS AWAY

Often when an interrupter comes along in whatever form—phone, office talker, someone with a problem—we find ourselves re-directed from our goal activities. If we are not aware of the time we are spending doing these non-track things, we can end the day completing nothing. What's worse, we seldom remember exactly how we got off track. **Be aware of interrupters, and keep them temporary, not re-directing.**

The second barrier to reaching our planning goals is much like what happened to the boy cleaning his room. When faced with so many challenges, we tend to have problems focusing on any of them and completing them.

The frustration that comes from this is shared by people in all professions and all lifestyles. Computer programmers always have to meet the many needs of the users in their companies. College students have many classes with tests and projects. Parents have jobs and children's needs.

TOO MANY THINGS TO DO

The case of too many things to do requires some serious analysis. If you are doing too many things, you are probably not doing any of them well. Then you get angry with yourself for not performing as well as you know you can. At work, your job may be too big for one person, in which case you might have to ask your boss to assign you help. In your home life, just the sheer number of people in a family multiplies house cleaning, bill paying, repairs, clothes buying, cooking, laundry, and errands, and these needs don't stop just because you work.

Solving this problem may require two approaches: planning better and/or delegating some tasks to someone else. Granted, both of these are often easier said than done. But your survival depends on your taking action to get yourself off the merry-go-round of a too hectic life. In case you haven't noticed, the horses on the merry-go-round are wood; you are not. **The best reason for managing your multiple responsibilities better is your own well-being.**

Your family members will rise to the task of doing their own laundry; co-workers will survive without your help on every task they are assigned, and your friends will get over it if you can't meet them for every gathering. Stop doing everything and train others around you to support what you do. Find a baby sitter who can help the kids with baseball or homework. Locate a temporary agency (they do all sorts of jobs these days) that can supply short-term help for your work. Look at your responsibilities and find ways to delegate at least some things.

The workplace and the home are, of necessity, team environments. Utilize the team. Analyze the tasks, the necessary track steps, and the resources; then decide how you will complete the tasks.

PERSONAL LIFE MANAGEMENT SKILL #3
COMPLETING THE TASKS

To complete your goals, you must be aware of time wasters and priority stealers. List below time wasters and priority stealers you often encounter when you try to accomplish goals. Then, prepare a strategy to prevent their interfering with what you need to do.

Example: Bill often sees me outside when I am doing a landscaping or building project and asks me to help him with something he wants to do right then. Response: "Sure, Bill, but right now I'm going to finish this deck.

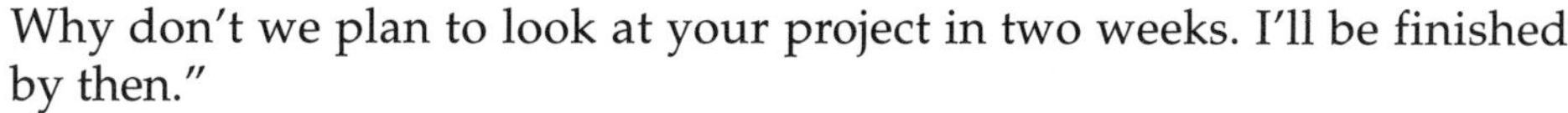

Why don't we plan to look at your project in two weeks. I'll be finished by then."

Time waster #1:

My new strategy for dealing with this time waster:

Time waster #2:

My new strategy for dealing with this time waster:

Building the well-managed life is not easy. But the necessity and the rewards are undeniable. Changing your old habits of being everyone else's best resource and of plunging into work without planning will require discipline at first. But, like other skills you are learning in this book, time and task management is very do-able. Plus, the reward is a happier and more relaxed *you.*

PERSONAL LIFE MANAGEMENT PLAN STEP #3

Prioritize Necessary Track

Secure Resources

Complete Tasks

Time and Task Organization Sheet

Goal to be completed:

	Necessary Track Step	Time needed
1.		
2.		
3.		
4.		
5.		
6.		

Resources needed:

Supplies:

Tools/equipment:

Human resources:

Resources I need to buy:	How much?	Where?

Resources I can make or rent:	How much?	Where?

People I know who can help:	Hire?	Friend or favor?

Potential time wasters:

1.

2.

3.

4.

5.

Strategies for time wasters:

1.

2.

3.

4.

5.

4 GATHERING INFORMATION AS LIFELONG LEARNING

"This is the information age."
"Get on the information highway."
"The world is changing; what you know will be obsolete in just a few years."

Trying to keep up with your business or just trying to stay informed about important aspects of your own life or work is becoming an ongoing challenge. However, most of what you knew five years ago is past history now. And, if you haven't added new ideas, skills, or information to your knowledge base, you are probably very much behind in your profession.

Lifelong learning is not just a buzzword or catchy phrase. It has become a way of living and thriving. The world is changing quickly, but information on that world, and the forces affecting it, is readily available **if** you know how to find and process it. By finding and using good information, you can live and work more effectively.

FINDING INFORMATION

Finding information is often confusing, frustrating, and overwhelming to people who have no idea how to go about it. If you have not been exposed to the wealth of resources in your own community, or if you have recently moved to a new city, you might be lost as to how to find services and suppliers.

Dirk and Sissy moved from their hometown to a city only 100 miles away. They felt sure that they would be able to find all that they needed simply by picking up the phone directory. Although the directory was an essential ingredient in the beginning, problems arose for them that were complicated and could not be answered simply by looking in the yellow pages.

Sissy had developed a pain in her left shoulder that hurt some of the time. She tried over-the-counter medications which only helped temporarily. She wanted to see a physician but did not know which specialty to consult.

Options included an orthopedist, a neurologist, or a chiropractor. She even considered a general practitioner. She was frustrated and realized how easy it was in her former home to count on advice from the network of professionals that she had grown to trust.

Dirk had attended a workshop that focused on problem solving. He and Sissy decided to use some of the techniques he had learned. They discussed the process over dinner and came up with a plan that would not only solve the physician dilemmabut would set a precedent for finding other resources they might need.

The steps they came up with were logic-based and took into account elements such as need, desire, finances, and ability.

- First state what you want to find/accomplish.
- List what you already know about the subject.
- List all resources that might be helpful, such as county agencies, reference librarians, human resource department at work, police departments, Red Cross, churches, and local information agencies.
- Make inquiry calls and gather information.
- Sort the information into options.

Using this formula, Dirk and Sissy gathered information about physicians in their area that might be good choices to treat shoulder problems. First, they narrowed down their list to the physicians that were on their side of town. Then they checked with the nearest hospital's physician referral service for doctors that seemed to fit what Dirk and Sissy were looking for.

They looked at the long-term view and also considered Dirk's desire to have a physician available to him if he needed one. They checked their finances and determined that they could manage an insurance deductible if they hadn't met it yet. The decision was to see a general practitioner. They picked one that was in the company insurance directory and was also recommended by Dirk's boss.

For them, what had been a difficult task in the beginning had turned out to be a learning experience which would benefit them when other situations came up in which they had to find resources.

Let us apply the above steps to other situations. If Bob were in need of information about a rent dispute, where would he begin? He would review his lease, then maybe check with the Better Business Bureau for past, unsolved complaints against his landlord. There might be a consumer advocate at his local newspaper or television station who could help.

Kelly is having financial problems. He might consult with his bank or make an appointment with the local consumer credit counsel. He might also buy a program for his computer that would help him organize his finances and develop a budget. He could also go to the library and obtain reading material on the subject.

Danielle is being stalked by an old boyfriend. What would she do? She might call the police for information on the laws regarding stalking. In addition, she could look in the local paper or on bulletin boards for a self-defense class. She could call an agency about hiring a bodyguard.

If the Dill family needed a plumber and did not know one, they could call a few phone listings and ask for references to be given by the plumber. They could ask friends or family members whom they use. They could check the advertisements in the newspaper and follow up with a call to the Better Business Bureau.

Russ and Amy want to stage a large wedding with all the trimmings. They could hire a wedding consultant, or search the latest publications on the subject for guidelines, or ask friends who have had experience, or use common sense combined with their own dreams.

Finding out about important things in one's life is often a matter of asking the right person. If you are a college student, besides the library, a major source of knowledge is the student services department. If you are employed, you can call upon the human relations department or the employee assistance representative. Others may simply check with libraries, state human services departments, clergy, police departments, telephone directories, 1-800- directories, and local chambers of commerce.

If you are in an emergency situation, call 911.

Assessment Activity #1

When you need to know something in a hurry, where do you usually look? Do you have a friend who is particularly well-informed on certain issues? Write down people you know who, themselves, are good sources of information.

1. Name:

   Source of information on:

2. Name:

   Source of information on:

Whatever your need is, you can find information if you know where to look. Information gathering for survival is most often a matter of knowing where to go to find answers to questions. Information gathering for school or work is much the same skill. For those instances, however, additional sources are available. On-line services, such as databases and the internet, will give you access to information on every topic you can think of through electronic mail, downloading services, bulletin boards, and several types of inter-active systems.

Some cities are starting to list all their services on local internet exchanges, and many, many colleges and universities are on the internet. An emerging type of access to internet is "commercenet." This will be the commercial exchange place for information about products and services. You will be able to look for a job or obtain airline flight information.

Anyone with a computer that has a modem in it (a modem allows your computer to call other computers over phone lines) can use the phone lines to gather and exchange all types of information. If you do not know anything about the internet, you would do well to find a course about it or visit a library that has it. Your future on the "information highway" depends on your understanding of this helpful and powerful tool.

You can find information on the internet or in books or magazines. You can also learn more about your world and the important ideas and events in it by attending seminars, classes, or lectures. But if you do not have good information-processing skills, you will probably not retain much of what you find or hear. Information is only as useful as your own ability to remember and apply it. Learning to program your brain for the maximum retention will help make you better prepared at work or school.

INFORMATION PROCESSING

Each of us remembers sitting around the reading circle or at a desk in school and being called on to read aloud. If we did well and read every word correctly, we learned two things: that reading every word is important and that reading was a good thing. If we didn't do well, we probably drew the conclusion right then and there that reading was difficult and that learning would have to come from other sources.

Interestingly enough, our schools offer very little guidance about information gathering after that first couple of years of teaching us to read (about second grade). Thus, some children figure out the "secrets" of fact finding in an efficient and time-effective way on their own. Other children grow into adulthood with an aversion to reading and a difficulty with locating information quickly and retaining it.

Whether you enjoy learning new ideas and procedures or not, you are living in an age where aggressive, lifelong learning is the key to career survival. Knowledge is indeed power, and the lack of knowledge about your job or the world is most certainly the opposite. Whether you are in a traditional college, technical school, or the work force, you have a daily need to process information.

Assessment Activity #2

Write down sources of information you have ready access to and that you use currently. Be sure to include professional magazines you read regularly as well as helplines or information services you use.

That information may be assignments in a textbook, a trouble-shooting guide for a new piece of equipment, steps in performing a work-related task, or facts about your company's products. Whatever it is, you are expected to gather and process it quickly and to retain it for future use. If you learned a method to do this while you were in school, you may have forgotten it by now. If you didn't learn it in school, now is the time.

As adults, we process information from the inside out, instead of the outside in.

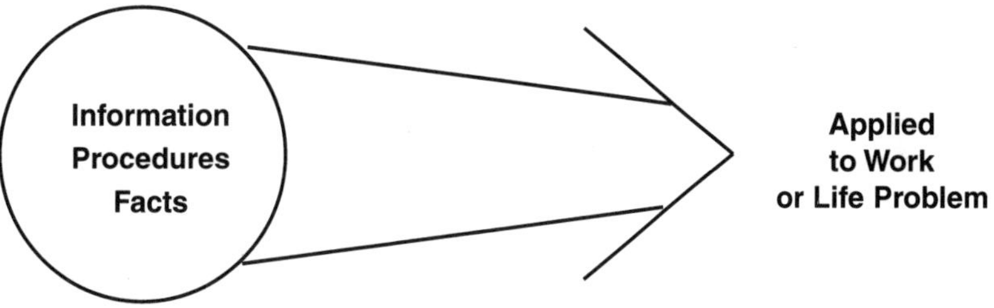

We take impressions, facts, perceptions, skills, and knowledge and apply them all day, every day to solving life's problems. We are expected to come up with creative solutions to work and home crises. Our brain begins to process in primarily one way. In a world that doesn't change much, this is not a problem. Unfortunately, ours is not that world. In the face of change, we need to constantly update intelligence on the world around us. This intelligence gathering makes us better equipped to meet the challenges that come at us daily and to recognize and capitalize on opportunities.

To do this requires us to program our brains for a new approach. Instead of screening out the myriads of impressions that come to us each day in ads, on the news, in conversation, and from our experiences, our minds have to be told to retain certain things because we need them. For example, if Kirby is to not go into overload, he must ignore and discount the many phone numbers that he hears on the television, radio, and other media. But if he is looking for car repair, and someone he knows offers him the number of a friend who is a reputable mechanic, he must program his information system to pay attention to and retain that number.

This works much like a computer or a filing system works.

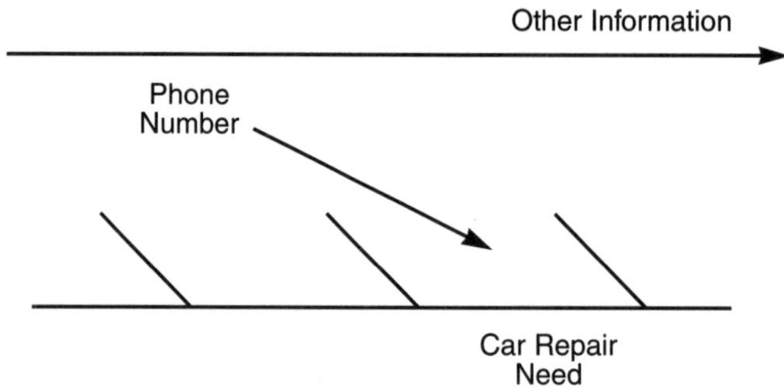

If you tell your brain you need to remember something, it will oblige you and not screen out important facts. If you do not specifically set up a reason to remember individual facts or ideas, your brain will select on its own with no useful pattern.

So, to accomplish efficient survival data gathering, you are going to have to engage in an inter-active process of listening and reading that meets your adult information needs. The techniques for this process are different than for your childhood tasks of this nature.

ACTIVE LISTENING

If your boss sends you to a training school at company expense for you to learn a new procedure for work, you had better learn it thoroughly. You will probably be asked to teach the others you work with what you have learned. For this task you will need to use active listening.

Step 1. Make sure you understand the purpose of the listening situation and the value of the information to you. Write down ahead of time the purpose and your information need.

Step 2. If you are a written information processor by nature (you learn best by reading), then set up columns on a piece of paper that are labeled with your information need.

The purpose of this seminar is to help us set up a local area network.

My need is to find out what trouble-shooting help might be given for our system.

Problems	Solutions	Help Available

If you are a visual person (you learn best by seeing pictures or diagrams of things), then you will need to set up a picture to help you collect the information and remember it.

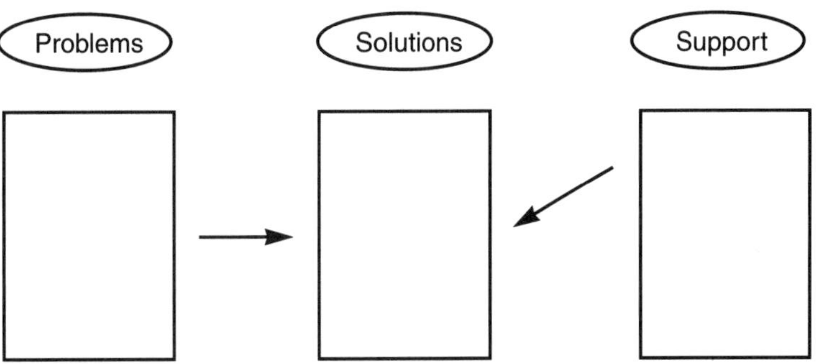

If you are a student who needs to study for tests, or a businessperson wanting to give a presentation, you might consider using one of the above approaches. The reason these visual note-taking methods help is that your concentration will begin to fade about two-thirds of the way down the page you are reviewing.

So, if you study by reading your notes only, you will likely miss test items or forget important facts that come from material found in the bottom one-third of your note pages. Pictures and columns help focus your eye and aid in helping you record what you want to remember. This technique helps you utilize the whole page without losing the bottom third.

Step 3. Wonder about what is being said. Your brain processes much faster than people talk, so it gets bored and eventually wanders off to something interesting. This is how you suddenly find yourself returning your attention to what is being said after several minutes of being "somewhere else." By actively wondering about what is being said, you keep focused on the topic. Also, this technique makes you process the information, so you are more likely to remember it.

For example

> "I wonder about the types of cable we will need for the network."

and

> "She mentioned a technical support staff. Are they by telephone or do they come out? If she doesn't say, I'll ask the question later."

Step 4. Take notes as you go, but don't let note taking interfere with listening. If you listen actively, you will understand the concept being discussed. And you will retain the idea long enough to write it down after the point is made.

Step 5. Repeat the main points in your head several times before moving on the next one. As was noted earlier, your brain processes very quickly and you will be able to do this a second or two.

Step 6. Ask questions whenever the speaker says it is okay. This could be during or at the end of a presentation. Either way, make sure the questions are relevant to your information needs but also be mindful of the needs of the group. Don't get too far afield with questions about your particular situation.

Step 7. After the presentation is over, immediately review the main points in your mind or in your notes to make sure you got the information you came there to receive.

PERSONAL LIFE MANAGEMENT PLAN SKILL #1
BECOME AN ACTIVE LISTENER

Describe below three situations where you can apply active listening skills to your advantage.

1.

2.

3.

What system will you use for these? (Examples: diagrams on notecards, a small notebook, pre-listening organizing charts, etc.)

Use the listening skills suggested here to teach yourself to be a better communicator. Observe political speakers, informative speakers, seminar leaders, religious speakers, salespeople, and television commercials. Look for not only the content of their communication, but also the techniques they use to make what they say sound believable and to make you want to act on or take in the information. Then, begin to use the same techniques in your own oral communication. Lifelong learning takes place every day if we avail ourselves of what information is offered over the many media in our society.

INTER-ACTIVE READING

Approaches to adult information gathering from print media are slightly different from "regular" reading. The first consideration is that you have very little time to devote to reading regardless of the importance of the information. Thus, the old reading circle approach of voicing every word is a waste of time. Nobody cares anymore if you can say every syllable.

Most adults read at less than 350 words per minute. If you have three textbook chapters, or two procedures manuals, or business proposals of 10,000 or more words each to read in a day, to study and prepare, or to be tested on, examine the practicalities of the situation. There isn't enough time at that rate to read all you need to read. Consequently, most people rely almost exclusively on the verbal media—talking and listening. Considering we retain less than 25 percent of what we hear after three weeks, this is a risky proposition. We are usually accountable for much more than that.

There are many techniques around to improve reading speed and comprehension: machine methods that flash lines of print at a set and increasing speed on a screen for you to read; courses where you learn to use special approaches to reading a page; and books about a psychological approach to reading. All of them have one thing in common, that is, they address the inefficient approaches we have learned and the bad habits we have developed in our reading.

But, if you understand certain things about information-gathering needs and human thinking patterns, you will quickly see how you can make dramatic improvements in a short period of time. Before we get too far into this discussion, take a half a moment (literally) to determine your own reading speed.

Assessment Activity #3: Determining Reading Speed

Instructions: Time yourself for 30 seconds while you read the passage below as quickly or slowly as you normally read. Then, circle your reading speed at the point where you stopped. (Note: It is much easier to do this if someone times you.)

Begin timing now:

Research Summary for Zero Emission Background Study

As a summary of the work of several people, the information following is
an overview of some of the research done to determine the degree of success
60 expected in marketing zero emission (electric) vehicles.

"Research studies say this. . . ." "Research studies say that. . . ." For
120 every topic or forecasting need there is some sort of research done. The
purpose of research is to add to information available for making decisions. It
180 should never be the sole basis for strategic planning or for forecasting. Products
have succeeded with the help of marketing research, and products have failed
240 with it. (Don't ask Coca-Cola how much they spent on researching the
disastrous "New Coke.") Forecasts alone, by their very nature, can completely
300 deny the effect of sound marketing strategy on consumers' willingness to buy
and are limited in their ability to fully determine risk or potential.

360 A good example of this is the decision for paint color on a car. Looking
at the figures for largest amount of paint sold, one would naturally conclude that
420 white was the best color to paint a car to make it sell well. In reality, though,
white is the choice for fleet vehicles in many areas and is not necessarily the first
480 choice of the buying public. In a quick survey of night students, ages 20–50, at a
local college, the color blue was the most popular, immediately followed by
540 black. The sample was largely male and largely engineers: both factors that
affected the interpretation of the outcome.

Interestingly enough, even in this non-scientific poll, an unexpected result
600 occurred: 31% said that stopping to put gas into their car was the most

bothersome element of having a vehicle. (The engine was 2nd with 27%.) So, being open-minded to a wide range of consumer responses often can lead to clear and helpful information.

Write your words-per-minute score here ;__________wpm.

BARRIERS TO SPEED AND COMPREHENSION

When we read at 300 words per minute, our brains get bored and our attention drifts, so that our eyes can actually arrive at the bottom of a page, but our brain doesn't remember reading any of it! One barrier becomes our own boredom. Thus, it is certainly logical to expect that reading faster improves your retention.

The concentration required to push yourself to read quickly all the time keeps you focused on what you are doing. That way, your brain doesn't have time to play. So, the notion that reading faster will decrease your ability to remember is invalid.

The second barrier is a bad habit that most of us have developed over the years of reading. Eye movement studies of people reading show that the eye constantly moves back up the page and goes over material time and time again. Keeping the eye moving down the page at a steady rate will probably double your reading speed the first few times you try it.

The third barrier is "soup can reading." This is similar to the old reading circle; you read every word, and somewhere in all those words you happen across something of value—eventually. You cannot afford to wait for "eventually" in the fast-paced world of information needs.

The final barrier discussed here (we will not address attention-deficit disorder or dyslexia, as those are specific reading barriers with therapeutic implications) will be that of non-inter-active reading. As was explained above in the illustration of information processing in the brain, if you do not read with a specific **purpose,** then most likely what you read will not be retained.

Purpose has a meaning here. "My boss told me to get through these specifications for Monday's job by tomorrow" is not purpose. Real purpose is you convincing your brain that what you are about to read has value to you. This is an act of conscious reading, of interacting with the material. **You accomplish inter-active reading by improving your concentration, using physical focus cues, quizzing yourself, and scribbling.**

Improvement Technique #1. Push yourself to move your eyes more quickly across the lines and down the page. The constant push will keep your concentration up. It will feel uncomfortable at first, as if you are not "reading" at all, but just getting your eyes to "hurry up" will give you a marked improvement.

Improvement Technique #2. Use an attention-getter to guide your eyes along the page. Some people use a small, colored ruler to slide down the page as they read. Some books, like textbooks and magazines, are very "busy" in their format. There are lots of pictures, ads, and other articles on the page. These can be very distracting and draw your concentration away from what you need to read and absorb.

A very good technique to prevent interference from distractions on the page is this: cut a square hole in a plain, white piece of paper. The size should be the width of the columns of print you are reading and about three inches or so long. Using this to slide down or across what you are reading will give a "window" effect, so you are drawn to the only interesting thing in your field of vision, the print.

Ideas about modern workplaces vary in
their view of the stay-at-home worker.
Some recommend the situation, others

Actually, even holding a pen on the page and moving it down while you read will help. The purpose is to keep your eye moving down the page and not going back up all the time.

Improvement Technique #3. Quiz yourself before, during, and after you read. A difficulty that we, as adults, have in learning new written material is that we seldom retain anything that we do not have to process immediately and for a purpose. If someone asks you a question about a political issue, for example, and you are embarrassed by not having any knowledge of the issue, then you will purposefully correct that situation. You will look up an article or ask someone. Likely, you will remember the answer to prevent further difficulties that could arise if you are asked again about the same topic.

The technique to help you gather information efficiently from printed material is quizzing. Before you read, think of questions you hope to have answered by the reading material. Then **read for the answers.** The easy proof that this works is looking up a phone number. You do not read every name on every page until you find John Smith on Halvern Lane. You, instead, program your brain to find the name on the street, then scan the page, skipping all names but his. Your eye will automatically pass over all the other Smiths and John Smiths and come to rest on your friend's name and address.

Quizzing after reading a fact you want to remember causes you to process the information through an additional path in your brain (the outgoing path as well as the incoming path) and increases your retention. Quizzing after each important idea you read reinforces in your mind that you **want** to know that information, and that your brain should not screen it out like it would an ad or a piece of unnecessary information.

Improvement Technique #4. Reading with a pen or pencil in hand and scribbling reactions to written material as you read it is an important part of effective adult information gathering. In elementary school we couldn't write in our books because they had to be returned and used the next year.

Now we are grown and we can buy our own books and magazines or photocopy a couple of pages at a time for our own use. That use is to acquire the important information about meaningful topics. So, scribble away in the columns, above the title, around pictures and charts. Underline or highlight critical ideas. Add notes on separate pieces of sticky paper.

These notes can be questions, disagreements with the facts or ideas proposed, expressions of confusion, or personal notes. What you write is not important. What is important is that you process by using the "wondering" technique suggested earlier in this chapter. Wonder on paper.

What Do You Think?

Look over the short selection below. From the title and the headings, create a diagram of the way you might set up your note-taking.

PLANNING A WORKING BUDGET

What People Don't Do

So many working people handle their daily tasks on the job quite well and responsibly, but their budgeting of personal finances lacks the same diligence.

This problem is common to both younger and older adults. Interviews with employees of a large consumer products company show that fewer than 20 percent have a savings or investment plan outside whatever their company provides. And, of those who use the company plan, few put aside the maximum amount allowed. In addition, there are only 18 percent who use any kind of consumer comparison guide or research to help them in purchasing products—even those purchases as large as a car. So, wage earners are not saving aggressively, and they are not using important and easily available reference material to ensure they obtain the best value for their money.

What They Should Do

It would appear that the best recommendation for anyone who wants to improve personal finances would be to not become involved in major get rich schemes or austere "buy nothing" purchase plans. Just saving a regular amount of money each month, no matter how small, will generate enough funds to finance a nice investment program that can grow into a hefty future source of income. In addition, just an hour or two of research into the quality of products in a given category will help prevent money being wasted on poor or overpriced products.

Set up your diagram(s) on a separate sheet of paper. Feel free, however, to write in the margins of this selection as you wish.

You will find that as you pattern yourself to read with a purpose and a plan, your concentration and memory for facts will improve. You will be able to program yourself to remember more of what you read in newspapers, professional publications, and general information sources.

PERSONAL LIFE MANAGEMENT PLAN SKILL #2
USE INTER-ACTIVE READING

Write below three written information sources that you would like to use to enhance your job or general knowledge level. These can be anything from textbooks for a class or seminar to instruction manuals.

1. Source 1:

2. Source 2:

3. Source 3:

What particular interactive reading skill will you apply to each of these?

1.

2.

3.

The tools you have developed in this chapter can be applied to any listening or reading situation to help you gain the most from what you see and hear. If you practice the skills regularly, they will become natural, and you will be able to use them without thinking. I suggest that you practice with newspapers, radio and TV newscasts, magazines, books, and any other listening or reading situations.

PERSONAL LIFE MANAGEMENT PLAN STEP #4

Become an Active Listener

Use Inter-Active Reading

UNIT II
PROGRESS CHECK AND AFFIRMATION

Dear Reader:

You've just completed the second step in your move toward a more successful and fulfilling life. Not only have you committed to changes, you have also gained the tools you need to begin to make those changes happen. You are organizing your time and tasks better, and you are able to find and retain information valuable to the attainment of your goals.

If you have not stopped yet to affirm your progress to yourself, do it now. Be nice to yourself during this process. If some topic seems difficult or uncomfortable to you, just pause and take a deep breath. Then, remind yourself of how well you are doing.

This is a discovery journey. You are discovering how really wonderful your life can become.

Sincerely,
B.W. and S. Mc.

STAGE THREE: DEVELOP CRITICAL SKILLS

5 Using Constructive Communication

It is amazing how miserable people can become because of what they say to themselves. Hardly a day goes by where I don't have people in my office who tell me how unhappy they are with their lives. When I ask about their internal self-talk, I find that they are subjecting themselves to a multitude of negative messages. They constantly bombard their psyches with unkind and scary thoughts which stir up worry, create stress reactions, and contribute to a feeling of being overburdened.

In addition, these same people are described by their friends and co-workers as "naysayers" or " wet blankets." They approach everything with a doomsday outlook. Common to their communication pattern are phrases such as, "That won't work" or "There are just too many obstacles for that to happen."They even project this to others, "You'll never get that promotion; someone else has seniority."

Resolving Negative Patterns

Negative communication with yourself and with others becomes a habit. It gives you a dismal view of the world at large, it destroys expectations, and it alienates other people who just don't want to hear pessimistic talk all the time.

The original cause for this doleful approach to life may have been a disappointment or even a tragedy. Though probably long forgotten, the event left behind a pattern of negativism. Note the example below.

Eileen, an insurance salesperson, created a dismal scene indeed when she talked about her work.

> "Our quota went up again this year, and the recession has really slowed down people's spending. I don't see how I can make it. No one is buying anything, let alone insurance. How can I pay my car note, my rent . . . ?"

As a single mother, she had an additional degree of worry other than just that connected with her work.

> "My son wants those expensive sports shoes all the kids are wearing. He's a teenager, and all that is important to him. I know he'll be crushed because we just can't afford them."

Not only is Eileen's negative talking causing her worry, she is even agitated on her son's behalf, adding his worry—which hasn't even materialized yet—to her own.

Bill, a 27-year-old journalism student, was deeply involved with a young woman with whom he grew up. He worried incessantly that she would become involved with other men. He obsessed about it every waking moment and often had sleepless nights wondering where she was and whom she was with.

Not only did he exhaust himself with his thinking patterns, he also exhausted her by his pressure for reassurance. She eventually grew weary of his behavior and did indeed leave him for another man. The end result for Bill was that his worry was justified by her leaving. He did not understand that it was his worry that drove her away.

Assessment Activity #1

Do I sometimes catch myself and others using negative talk? Write below examples of negative talk you have used with yourself and with others. Also, record examples of negative talk you hear others around you using.

1. Negative things I say to myself:

   a.

   b.

2. Negative things I say to others.

   a.

   b.

3. Negative things I hear others say.

   a.

   b

After doing this activity, you might notice that there are others around you who have patterns of negative talk as well. Some people who would ordinarily have a positive life view and attitude find themselves in negative environments. These environments can affect the way we feel about our work and relationships.

In both Eileen's and Bill's cases negative thinking and worry led to unpleasant results. The following discussion introduces you to strategies that will help you cope with undesirable conditions in a positive way.

The negative thinkers described above have had much practice. Plus, they usually aren't even aware that they are the source of their own misery. They tend to blame their unhappiness on everything but their negative thinking styles.

Negative communicators say: "If only __________would happen, I could be happy."

Those who use negative communication also have negative expectations and thinking patterns. They wait for life to change rather than begin to change what they can about life. They usually wind up "waiting" most of their lives. And, as for those who arrive at good fortune, they often cannot enjoy it because they have programmed themselves negatively for so long that they don't know how to stop and enjoy it.

Negative thinking is most often a product of our past experiences. It is a process which is clearly out of our conscious awareness. We learn these patterns as children and continue to repeat them. Because we are usually very young when these things occur, we do not have the intellectual capacity to question the critical judgments or the unflattering comments that we are hearing. We take the information as absolute fact and proceed to operate on these ideas for years to come. The total effect of this is the development of a negative self-view. It is impossible to look constructively and positively on the world through eyes shaded by a negative self-view. These patterns become ingrained in our unconscious thinking and control our lives.

Assessment Activity #2

Sometimes the negative judgments or comments we received in the past follow us into the present without our being aware of their effect. Write in the space below any negative talk that was directed at you by parents or other authority figures in the past.

1.

2.

3.

4.

The accumulated effects of this negative thinking on us are dramatic. We become stressed out, self-esteem decreases, confidence fades, and we are unable to stay focused on our goals. Experiencing a sense of hopelessness about our lives, we feel powerless and struggle to gain some control. This struggle drains us emotionally and causes us to unconsciously create situations that go badly. As in the case of Bill, adverse thoughts often become self-fulfilling prophecies, and the cycle of negativity continues.

One of the most powerful weapons against negative thinking is its counterpart, positive thinking, reflected in constructive communication. Just as doleful or dismal thoughts become habits, upbeat and bright thoughts and communication can become a personal operating style. Following are the steps for breaking the habit:

1. **Listen to what you say to yourself and note how you react to life events.**

   This will make you aware of the extent of the negative habit in your own life.

"I must be a real idiot for leaving my wallet at home."

or

"Oh, no, the boss wants to see me; what have I done wrong?"

2. **Decide the specific negative patterns you would like to change.**

"I'm noticing a lot of self-criticism, and I'd like to stop doing that."

or

"I notice I automatically assume the worst. I would like to stop assuming I am incompetent or at fault all the time."

"Whenever something new comes up at work, everyone, including me, seems to expect the worst."

3. **Design a new way of communicating to yourself that reflects the positive.**

"I forgot my wallet. That's the first time in four years I've done that. Not bad! Now, where might I have left it?"

or

"The boss wants to see me. Wonder what he needs?"

4. **Practice operating as a positive self-talker. Expect positive outcomes.**

Not "I'll never get the boss to notice my good work"

but "How can I get the boss to notice my good work?"

Not "Alan won't call. He's always too busy for me."

but "I haven't heard from Alan. Maybe I should call him."

5. **Become an agent of constructive communication in your circle of friends or co-workers.**

"Frank, can we hear your plan for solving the problem instead of how damaging you think it is?"

"Melissa, you sound like you are sad much of the time. Can I help, or is this private?"

"You know, we all seem to be hypercritical of this professor. Can we just stop all that negative talk and figure out a way to do better in his class?"

BUILDING CONSTRUCTIVE COMMUNICATION

In the **Personal Life Management Plan** for this chapter you will learn to use constructive communication by building positive self-talk. There are three very basic steps towards alleviating the habit of negativity:

- Eliminate negative talk to yourself.
- Adopt a constructive vocabulary and operating style.
- Build a constructive communication environment.

Positive talkers recognize the complainer's rut and learn to avoid it. Some people can be negative about a sunny, springtime day. They have just fallen into the pattern of pointing out the downside of everything. Monitoring your speech and considering yourself a source of positive comments will make your day go better, your social relations seem brighter, and your work become a challenge instead of drudgery.

Remember, much of the negative outlook people project comes from a negative self-view. Considering that the source of this low expectation self-view is often from the messages sent by others, you will profit by examining each of these messages now that you are an adult.

The activity that follows will require you to look at negative messages you have received in the past and evaluate them from a positive, adult perspective. Be careful to stay in a positive mode while responding.

PERSONAL LIFE MANAGEMENT SKILL #1
ELIMINATE NEGATIVE TALK

Now that you've examined your negative self-talk, both messages from the past and negative habits of the present, target specific statements which were unflattering or critical that you wish to eliminate.

Example:

Negative comment: "You never get anything right" (from your third grade teacher).

Positive self-view response: As an adult I am quite reliable in completing tasks. In the third grade I was a child still learning. That person was wrong. I want to eliminate that from my self-talk.

(Remember that one of the reasons you are reading this book is that you realize you are developing yourself into the kind of person you want to be. Affirming progress on this path is an important part of directing your destiny.)

1. Negative comment:

   Positive self-view statement:

2. Negative comment:

   Positive self-view statement:

3. Negative comment:

   Positive self-view statement:

A characteristic of constructive communication is its expectation for success. Each problem becomes a problem-solving exercise, not a stress inducer. Positive self-talkers find ways to define success in their daily activities: homemakers can congratulate themselves on managing multiple tasks; construction workers can take pride in their daily contribution to the home they are building; programmers can give themselves a pat on the back because the systems they manage continue to provide service under their care.

PERSONAL LIFE MANAGEMENT SKILL #2
ADOPT CONSTRUCTIVE STYLE

As you look at the challenges and frustrations of your daily life, begin to re-design your responses to reflect positive expectations. For each of the difficulties you run into, formulate a sentence that will clearly reflect the positive side of the picture. Use present tense to create these responses.

Example: The phone system is acting up and cutting customers' calls short.
Positive response : I can call some of our larger accounts to make sure they aren't having problems today.
Example: You feel you are overloaded with responsibilities.
Positive response: I can organize my day in order to finish my work.

1. Challenging situation:

   Positive response:

2. Challenging situation:

   Positive response:

3. Challenging situation:

   Positive response:

Once you begin approaching communication in a more empowered and effectual way, you may notice how easy it is to be infected or influenced by negative talk around you. If your friends constantly criticize each other or you, then that is creating a negative environment. Often they will tell you, when they say something unkind or sarcastic, "I'm just telling it like it is." Perhaps they are, or maybe, instead, they are only telling one side, the negative.

I was sitting with a group of friends at lunch just recently, and they all seemed to be whining about the amount of work they had to get done by a deadline. As the lunch progressed, I began to notice my own attitude taking a nose dive into the complaining mode. By the time I left, my former good mood had deteriorated to a glum, low energy frame of mind. I even caught myself in a negative response. The receptionist remarked that the weather was lovely, and I instantly responded, "Yeah, but it will probably rain tomorrow." Negativism is contagious!

What Do You Think?

Renee is unhappy with her job. She loves the work as an accountant, but is becoming affected by the working environment. People complain a lot, and no one seems enthusiastic or motivated to do a good job. A co-worker says that the boss is too demanding. Another says that the workers are underpaid. Renee's office mate confides that she is looking for another job because she is not appreciated for the work she does. Renee decides to talk with the boss and recommend some changes to make the office more productive.

What are some "constructive talk" ways Renee can make these recommendations?

Several approaches are possible in dealing with negative environments created by friends or co-workers. **One approach might be to de-fuse the effect the negativism has on you.** This is easily accomplished by your recognizing the dismal talk for what it is and laughing about it to yourself. "I can't believe how negative Angela sounds today!"

Another way of handling a negative environment is stay away from the "gloom and doom" people and attach yourself to more positive and upbeat individuals. You will be amazed at how your energy level and your whole demeanor are affected positively by surrounding yourself with people who use constructive communication.

Finally, if retreat is not possible, then **you may want to confront the "gloomy Gus" types and expose their negativism.** Sometimes people do not realize the habit they have let themselves fall into. You may want to do this in the framework of attempting to improve conditions for everyone by choosing to approach conversation constructively.

PERSONAL LIFE MANAGEMENT SKILL #3
BUILD A CONSTRUCTIVE ENVIRONMENT

Describe below two situations where the environment you operate in is characterized by negativism. Then, outline a plan to address this and change the situation to a more constructive one. Use one of the techniques described above.

Situation #1:

Plan for change:

Situation #2:

Plan for change:

In summary, positive thinking, demonstrated by constructive communication, is an effective tool to reverse negative directions in your life. However, it is your responsibility to utilize the tool in creating the life you really want for yourself. Changing old habits requires time. It has been my experience that it takes approximately four to six weeks to replace old patterns with new ones. So persistence will bring you ever closer to the destiny you choose.

PERSONAL LIFE MANAGEMENT PLAN STEP #5

Eliminate Negative Talk

Adopt a Constructive Communication Style

Build a Constructive Communication Environment

Replacing Worrying with Problem Solving

Everyone worries about something, sometime. Aunt Eleanor worries about her friends dying. Ben at age six worries if he will be tall enough to play basketball. Parents worry about children in day care. Salespeople worry about meeting quotas. Some even worry that they are worrying too much! It's not the worry that creates difficulties; it's the way we worry that can sometimes prevent us from moving forward toward our goals.

Learned Worry Styles

There are many ways in which we worry about problems. If we look at our own approach, we might determine that we use more than one style. Our individual worry style usually develops from our observations of others as they react to problems. Maybe your style came from watching your father pace the floor or seeing your brother bite his nails.

The way you approach problems is probably learned, and a new, more effective method of addressing the challenges you face can be learned also. Some worry patterns are merely ineffective in solving difficult situations. Some, however, can be quite damaging. Overeating, drinking, excessive television watching are all easily recognizable as negative worry patterns.

Symptoms such as irritability, tension, headaches, sleeplessness, upset stomach, and fatigue are not always traceable to one incident but are rather the result of endless worrying over a period of time. Relationships, health, and jobs can all suffer when the symptoms of worry become chronic conditions. High blood pressure, chronic constipation, ulcers, depression, and phobias can usually be linked to damaging responses to life's dilemmas. To avoid this painful path, we must look at our styles of worrying and develop more effective strategies for addressing problems.

Assessment Activity #1

For today, take a self-inventory of what your body is doing when you feel upset about something that is happening. Write your observations in the space below. If possible, record anyone else you remember who worries in the same way.

Observation #1. I notice I am

____

I remember seeing ______________________ do this.

Observation #2. I notice I am

____

I remember seeing ______________________ do this.

Observation #3. I notice I am

____

I remember seeing ______________________ do this.

SOURCES OF WORRY

Worry comes from problems. Not everything that is a problem to one person is a problem to another, so judging your problems by others is seldom a good idea. A colleague of mine ran an interpersonal skills workshop with a group of models. These women, all beautiful to most of us, expressed concern over their lack of perfection: " My left cheekbone is nearly one-eighth inch off, so they will only take three-quarter shots of my face" or "I can not go swimming with you today; that woman over there is much taller than I am and looks so much better." Vanity? It would seem so to us, but for people who succeed or fail by their looks, these are very real concerns.

Often, worry comes from things over which we have no control: forced layoffs, weather conditions, political changes, management changes, aging processes. Though certainly these situations are inevitable, they are problems only if you have no method for dealing with them as they come.

One 35-year-old client of mine obsessed over whether her husband would die before her. The worry became such a habit that she was not even aware of its effects. She began to have vague physical symptoms that were painful but not readily traceable to any medical condition. Under therapy she noted that her mother had been a worrier, and she began to tie her own behavior to that she had seen in her mother.

Reality showed that her husband was in good health and was from a long-lived family. Further exploration, however, revealed that her father had died suddenly when she was a child. She had felt frightened and out of control at the time. The behavior she saw in her mother, combined with her leftover fear, created a pattern of unnecessary worry. After understanding this, she became more realistic about her husband's mortality and was able to focus on present conditions which she could solve.

Other sources of worry include those things over which we have control. A concern over being laid off could lead to your taking a class in career management or upgrading your professional skills. Worry about your children could motivate you to seek family counseling. It is rarely the worries which motivate us to positive action that are hurtful; it is those that paralyze us and prevent us from seeking solutions that are harmful. Solving problems in these areas requires concentration and effort, but good results are possible.

Assessment Activity #2

Below, list four things you are worried about right now. After each one describe the worry in terms of Current (C) or Long-term (L). Also, try to classify each as Under my Control (UC) or Not under Control (NC).

	WORRY	C	L	UC	NC
1.					
2.					
3.					
4.					

You will be amazed that no matter how complex the problem is or what source the problem comes from, you can use clear, constructive thinking to eliminate the helpless feeling the worrier so often experiences. **Critical thinking, in the form of good problem-solving skills, will free you from the helplessness of having no way out of life's unpleasantness when it occurs.**

Having a positive approach to problems and critical thinking skills that lead you to good solutions will make you feel stronger and more in control of your life. As you feel more adept at handling tough situations as they come up, you will experience less stress and less inclination to worry. You will begin to manage your life from a base of power rather than a base of fear. Following is the **Personal Life Management Plan** for using problem-solving skills.

USING CRITICAL THINKING TO ISOLATE THE PROBLEM

The beginning of the solution to any problem is isolating exactly what the problem is. That seems easier than it is in practice and takes considerable skill.

An example is one many people have faced at some point in their lives. Marcus's phone bill and the rent are both due, and his girlfriend's birthday is coming up. His income is small because he is a student and works only part-time. He says the problem is:

> "I don't have enough money."

Actually, the problem is more complex than that. Until Marcus looks at the situation critically, he is not going to be able to effectively solve the problem.

A detailed definition of the problem would look like:

Need present for girlfriend—she will get feelings hurt if present is not nice.

Must pay rent—will be evicted and have no place to live if rent is not paid.

Must pay phone bill—phone would be cut off and part-time job involves telemarketing from home, so job would be lost.

Marcus worries that his girlfriend might leave him if he "forgets" her birthday.

Others might think Marcus is "cheap" or "poor" if he doesn't get a nice present.

Marcus does not want to ask parents for extra money because that would take away from his independence.

Marcus has no other source of income because work and school take all his time.

This analysis shows that Marcus's real problem is that he feels like he must live up to all sorts of other people's expectations: his girlfriend's, his parents', and other people he knows. If he begins to look at the "problem" from this angle, he might realize that his relationships are not quite as fragile as he perceives. His girlfriend might not actually be expecting an expensive gift; she might, instead, just want some uninterrupted time with him. It also might not hurt for Marcus to have a discussion with her about money and their relationship.

So **the first step in isolating a true problem for solution is to think critically about what the problem really is.** This is true for relationships, as noted above, and it is even more true on the job. In a manufacturing plant, Rosalind, the human resources director, noted that absenteeism and turnover were especially high in one department. She concluded that employee motivation was the problem and began looking at incentive programs that would cost the company many thousands of dollars to implement.

Just before she contracted for the program, Rosalind talked with an employee in the department over coffee. When she asked about the morale in the department, the employee responded emotionally. The manager, apparently, would quite often, and for no apparent reason, verbally attack employees at random. The work environment was so tense that no one wanted to come to the plant knowing they would have to be around that volatile manager.

Rosalind followed up on the situation and found out that the manager had a chemical abuse problem. He was placed on leave for six weeks and was referred to a company-sponsored rehabilitation program for addiction. In his absence, productivity immediately improved, and absenteeism dropped. The problem was not the employees; it was the manager. The company almost spent many thousands of dollars on the wrong problem.

What Do You Think?

Larry has been a cross-country truck driver for 7 years. He has a 4-year-old daughter and a new baby boy. Larry took the job right out of high school. He has no other job experience or special skills. He would like to get off the road to spend more time with his family.

What is Larry's real problem?

What are some possible solutions?

What would be Larry's reward for a good solution?

Isolate what the "real" problem is before seeking alternative solutions. As in the case of Marcus above, he was worried about a problem that may or may not have been the true source of his difficulty. When we worry, it is often because we feel powerless to solve the problem we see at hand. Worry should be a trigger for us to go into a problem-solving mode. **Defining problems is the first step to eliminating worry.**

PERSONAL LIFE MANAGEMENT SKILL #1
ISOLATE THE PROBLEM

Take two sources of worry you currently have. For each, write down several possible views of the problems that could be causing these worries. Then, look at these alternative views and write a single, specific problem statement.

Worry #1:

Alternative views of the problem:

Specific problem statement:

Worry #2:

Alternative views of the problem:

Specific problem statement:

Once you have isolated the problem as:

"The problem is the lack of money for bills" or
"The problem is the way you ignored me around your friends" or
"The problem is how hurt I get when you don't seem to care about my feelings"

you are ready to begin seeking solutions.

THINKING CREATIVELY TO GENERATE SOLUTIONS

Here is where you need to become creative in your thinking. Concepts such as the telephone and the microwave oven did not come out of conventional thinking. They arose from an inventor's ability to visualize new solutions to existing problems.

Good solutions come from those alternatives generated from the imagination, not from everyday thinking. Also, the best solution is rarely the first or third you come up with; more likely it will be the twenty-fifth. Imaginative solutions lead to creative problem solving, and it this skill that gets you out of the problem rut. The rule for coming up with solutions in this part is that there are no rules. The more creative and outlandish the idea seems, the closer you may be to finding your answer.

PERSONAL LIFE MANAGEMENT SKILL #2
GENERATE SOLUTIONS

Part 1. Practice thinking creatively by doing the following. Remember, more ideas lead to better ideas. Warm up for this by writing down every use you can think of for old milk cartons. Give yourself five minutes and work toward a list of ten or more.

Part 2. Now, pick a problem you have isolated for yourself to work on. List *at least* five ideas you can think of for solutions. Then, take a break for five minutes and list five more. Don't worry if they are workable or not, just pat yourself on the back for your creativity, especially if you go over five in either set.

Problem:

Solutions set 1:

Solutions set 2:

Since you are now expanding your view of problems and of possible solutions, it is time to analyze what you have come up with and begin to narrow down your choices.

ANALYZING TO WEED OUT THE LEAST WORKABLE

Once options are generated, it is time to rule out ones that have negative consequences. Remember that you want positive outcomes in your life, and problem solving should help you find new ways to make things go better for you. Of the positive options you have left, investigate what would be involved in carrying each out. The example below will guide you.

A shipping manager had to cut the budget in his department by $35,000 for the next year. He had several options:

fire a $35,000 per year employee
fire two part-time clerical people
cut hours on three hourly employees
offer reduced time/reduced pay to employees
cut out training and incentive programs for the year
suggest early retirement option to old-timers
cut benefits
eliminate achievement awards and lunches
dock pay for sick leave
increase productivity to offset losses
drop dependents from benefits plan
eliminate the college co-op program

He saw only two positive solutions for his purposes. He investigated the numbers of people who had small children or live-in elderly parents to see how many might actually welcome reduced hours in order to have more time to spend on family business. Looking at the other side of the issue, he recognized that the order to cut costs was due to productivity losses. Increases in productivity might eliminate the need for the cut altogether.

PERSONAL LIFE MANAGEMENT SKILL #3
WEED OUT THE LEAST WORKABLE

Take the problem solutions you have developed in Skill #2 and eliminate the least workable. (Note: you might want to investigate the steps it would take to implement several before you decide what can work and what can't.) You can ask for information from others (don't ask for their solutions, just gather any knowledge they may have on *your* solutions).

1. Solution alternative #1:

   I could make this work by :

2. Solution alternative #2:

   I could make this work by:

3. Solution alternative #3:

   I could make this work by:

So, you see, going all around a problem with no limits on what you can consider can lead you to several options that can create positive outcomes. Investigating the workability of more than one option might surprise you. Something you thought could never happen might actually become a reality through your efforts. The final step then puts your ideas and investigation to work.

ACTING TO IMPLEMENT YOUR CHOICE

Action is the key to lowering stress in difficult situations. Problems sometimes paralyze us with their size, so we become inactive, feeling powerless to help. Positive activity becomes the great helper. The mere carrying out of options can give us a feeling of contributing to a solution instead of being ground down by circumstances.

Perhaps your solution requires a little more asking, planning, and researching to be effectively implemented. Don't stop. Go ahead: ask, plan, and research. You will feel more positive and will thus be more motivated to keep at the task of carrying out your ideas. Even if the first solution you pick proves imperfect, you have other good ones you have already thought up and investigated. Get going!

PERSONAL LIFE MANAGEMENT SKILL #4
IMPLEMENT YOUR CHOICE

Now that you have a good solution to your problem, implement it. Then, return to this exercise and write below the outcome of that activity. If it worked as you desired, go on to Skill #5. If not, choose another of your top three and implement that one. Record the outcome.

How solution was implemented:

Outcome:

CONGRATULATING YOURSELF TO AFFIRM YOUR ACHIEVEMENT

Every problem you solve is an achievement. Enjoy your success and let each success support you in your next challenge. Never forget to give yourself credit for the growth you are experiencing. Each chapter you read in this book and each activity you do puts you ahead of those who are still lost in inactivity, overcome by a life out of control. You are learning to steer your way out of storms. There will always be more storms, but you will learn from each one, and the next will be easier, as will the next, and the next.

PERSONAL LIFE MANAGEMENT SKILL #5
CONGRATULATE YOURSELF

For the problems you have worked on in this chapter, list below each one you have now found a solution for and tell why it was a good solution. This exercise will allow you to affirm the good you are doing for yourself by becoming a careful problem solver.

Solution #1:

This solution was good because:

Solution #2:

This solution was good because:

Solution #3:

This solution was good because:

Many people think that problem-solving ability and creativity belong only to a few gifted individuals. Actually, by using the skills you have learned in this chapter, you will improve your ability to work through problems toward positive solutions. Up to now you may have made decisions on "gut" or intuition. From this point on, however, you can add to your intuition a good, solid approach to life's challenges and replace worry with the power of your new skill.

PERSONAL LIFE MANAGEMENT PLAN STEP #6

Isolate the "Real" Problem

Generate Solutions

Weed Out the Least Workable

Implement the Best Solution

Congratulate Yourself

7 CONFRONTING CONFLICT

Conflict is a part of everyone's life. Yet few people feel that they handle conflict well. Part of the difficulty is that growing up, we seldom get the opportunity to learn positive conflict resolution. We all remember seeing conflicts; these are natural in every family. Probably, though, you do not remember seeing conflicts resolved. In this chapter you will learn where conflicts come from and how to recognize them at their source. You will also come to understand your own and others' reactions to conflict. Finally, you will learn a positive approach to truly resolving the difficulties in your life that result from conflict.

CONFLICTING NEEDS AS A SOURCE OF CONFLICT

Conflicting needs are a fundamental source of discord in relating to others. Any time my need is different from yours, we have a conflict to some degree. How we treat that conflict is subject to our learned approach to conflict, degree of need, kind of relationship, strength of emotion, and level of self-esteem. Thus, if the conflict of need is in an area where I do not have a strong emotional involvement, I may be calm and logical in my handling of the situation. If the other person involved is someone I like and respect, then I will likely be highly motivated to seek a positive solution that is acceptable to both of us.

But, on the other hand, if my feelings are hurt, or if I feel the other person's need is overbearing and unfair, then I may react with anger. Conflicts can be quite volatile under these situations, but they do not have to be. The situation below illustrates a simple need conflict.

Tom and Donnie live next door to each other. Tom works the early shift, 7 to 3, and Donnie works the graveyard shift, 11 to 7. In addition to his job,

Donnie keeps his daughter until his wife gets home from work at 1. So, bedtime for Donnie is about 2 P.M. Tom likes to mow his lawn when he gets off work. The noise from the mower awakens Donnie.

Donnie's need: to sleep within a certain schedule.

Tom's need: to mow early so he can spend time with his children when they get home at 4.

There is a need conflict. Donnie knows that if he speaks to Tom, there is the potential for conflict. So, knowing this, Donnie might act in any of several ways depending on his learned approach to conflict.

- Donnie may not say anything in order to avoid creating bad feelings.
- Donnie might yell and threaten Tom, or make noise early to waken him.
- Donnie could become depressed over his inability to control the situation.

Assessment Activity #1

In the situation above, which action of Donnie's might most closely resemble your own approach to conflict?

Your approach is:

An example of this might be:

APPROACHES TO CONFLICT

In the discussions following, we will look at these ways of responding to conflict: **evasion, anger, sadness.**

EVASION

Some evade altogether situations that might lead to conflict. A wife finds out her husband is cheating and keeps up appearances, pretending everything is okay. Employees will keep bad news away from the boss to avoid a scene. Customers sometimes will keep defective products, so they do not have to assert themselves to a customer service person. This pattern of evasion is learned very early in our lives and supported over time.

In the case of safety issues it is mandatory that a child obey parents without question. This is where the pattern starts. When a truck is speeding toward a child who has wandered out into the street, there is no time for a lengthy discussion on the freedom to cross streets at will. This is certainly not the time to instruct a child in problem-solving techniques; haste and instant reaction are necessary for safety. The child, however, may read a demand for obedience as a message that she is incapable of solving problems that affect her.

Those who grow up in troubled families learn to tread lightly around many issues to prevent a flare-up of anger in the household and the effects of that anger on others. These individuals feel that by evading conflict, they can prevent problems from erupting. Thus, they never learn how to address issues and see a conflict through to a positive resolution.

These early patterns set up an unconscious mechanism that causes a withdrawal from conflict of any kind. In adult life, then, conflict avoidance becomes a pattern that we are not even aware of. This evasion reaction becomes ingrained in us and causes us to resist, often at great cost, any entry into a disagreement or conflict.

Some people go to such great lengths to avoid these situations that they make themselves physically sick. Todd was taught all his life never to argue with authority, to just "take it." So, eventually, after years of unresolved conflicts at his job, he began having stomach pains like those associated with ulcers. He came to me at the suggestion of his medical doctor. His case is not an uncommon one.

At first, he was reluctant to talk about the problems causing his stress. "I don't know what you can do for me. I've just got some stuff that I have to work out." The discussions that followed did bring out some rather serious conflicts Todd was having at his job. When I asked him if he had discussed any of these with his supervisor, he responded, "When I was growing up, it was always, 'Keep your mouth shut and do what you're told.'" Consequently, Todd held inside the anger from every conflict he avoided. His learned conflict avoidance style eventually showed up in the form of a potentially serious health problem.

Assessment Activity #2

Take a moment to recall the kinds of conflict in your upbringing. What do you remember about the way they were handled and how they made you feel?

This evasion approach may cause us a great deal of emotional pain. **In avoiding conflict, we avoid the depth of close relationship.** As long as people in the world think differently, there will be variations and conflict to some degree. Part of the richness of a relationship is learning about the sometimes opposite views others hold. We broaden our own thinking by exposing ourselves to alternative views.

Conflict is a method of enhancing this process. Conflict is a fact of life. It is as natural as breathing, loving, or eating. Once we understand that **conflict is an important part of emotional and intellectual growth,** we then relieve ourselves of the dread we feel when we approach and deal with it. All the energy that used to be spent in worrying about or evading conflict situations can instead be directed toward positive resolutions.

Assessment Activity #3

Write down examples of conflict situations you have been in where you attempted to evade the conflict. Tell how you handled the situation.

Conflict situation #1:

I attempted to evade this situation by:

Conflict situation #2:

I attempted to evade this situation by:

ANGER

Another way of responding to conflict is anger. Our bodies respond to anger the same way they do to a life-threatening situation. Adrenaline causes the heart to frantically pump blood to the muscles. The stomach churns. All that energy has to go somewhere, and sometimes it translates into angry blowups.

One of the sources of anger is emotional hurt. When self-esteem is damaged, our mind translates that into an attack at some level and responds—

sometimes with hostility. If someone criticizes your clothes, you might feel indignant and want to answer the criticism smartly with anger. You can also get angry from the hurt of embarrassment, as in the practical joke. Any of these situations can lead to a highly charged conflict that will be difficult to resolve because of the emotions involved.

Assessment Activity #4

Write down conflict situations that you can recall where anger was the response to conflict. Try to identify the source of the anger for yourself or for the other person. Label the type of anger as emotional pain, physical pain, or lack of control.

Conflict situation #1:

Source of anger:

Conflict situation #2:

Source of anger:

What you may notice is that your anger comes out of the circumstances introduced above. If anger is your conflict style, then you are indeed experiencing a lot of stress because of the way you are approaching conflict in your life.

SADNESS

Another possible reaction to conflict is sadness or depression. Some people just shut down and feel powerless. Instead of meeting the conflict head on and resolving it, they will retreat within themselves and consistently give in when a conflict occurs. This continual denial of their own needs in the face of others' needs eventually mounts up. They begin to feel an unexplainable sadness, and may even suffer from serious depression.

Some of this sadness comes from being powerless to act as they feel they should. When a verbally abusive husband consistently screams at his wife, often the male child will withdraw and become depressed. He feels he should protect his mother and cannot. In a job situation you might become sad when you have a conflict with your co-worker or friend and you do not resolve it positively.

Assessment Activity #5

Recall conflicts, both past and recent, where the outcome created a feeling of sadness in you.

Conflict situation #1:

Source of sadness:

Conflict situation #2:

Source of sadness:

None of the responses mentioned to this point are constructive ways to handle a conflict.

HANDLE CONFLICT CONSTRUCTIVELY

Conflict resolution is for the person who genuinely cares about both self and others, and is motivated to resolve, rather than temporarily stifle, conflict. This requires a certain amount of maturity. There are several techniques for conflict resolution that have been used effectively for a number of years.

The easiest way to resolve conflict is to do it from your own sense of inner strength. When you are self-assured, you have a sense of strength about yourself that allows you to back off a step from a situation that could be volatile. By taking one step back, you initially give yourself an opportunity to detach somewhat from the intensity of the conflict.

The more you get caught in the intensity, the more your emotions become hooked into the scene. If that happens, you are less likely to be able to think clearly . You will also be less likely to come up with solutions that could be suitable to both parties. **So, the first step is to back off and get a handle on your own emotions.** (Note: An effective way to do this is to ask yourself what emotions you are experiencing at the time. For example you might say to yourself, "Am I angry, or embarrassed, or hurt, or ashamed, or . . . ?")

PERSONAL LIFE MANAGEMENT SKILL #1
HANDLE EMOTIONS

Over the next two days take note of the times you become emotional in a conflict. Say to yourself, "I recognize I am angry (or hurt, or embarrassed), and I need to look past my reaction to see the real problem in this conflict."

Conflict situation:

I recognize that I am ______________________________

I think_________________________ might be one of the problems.

After you have taken your emotional step back, try to listen very carefully to what the other person is saying. Listen so carefully that you can repeat exactly what that person has said without missing a word. This kind of listening allows you to enter into the other person's world.

When you do this, you learn something vitally important about the other person's inner workings and needs. You may even choose to clarify what is being said, "I don't understand exactly what makes you feel so angry about this situation." **The second step is to listen with great attention to detail.**

PERSONAL LIFE MANAGEMENT SKILL #2
LISTEN TO DETAIL

The next time you find yourself in a conflict situation (yours or someone else's), listen carefully to what is being said. Look for fact (issues) statements and feeling (emotions) statements. Write several of these below.

Conflict description:

Feeling statements:

Fact statements:

(Note: Good listening is a key element in effective conflict handling. It is a good habit to cultivate.)

Next, you can share with the other person your feelings about the conflict. Ask him or her to give you equal time to do so. Assert your needs in a straightforward and non-emotional way. This conveys that your view of the situation is as valid as the other person's .

If Sharon feels that her car was not repaired properly, her first response might be to avoid a confrontation and pay her bill anyway. Instead, she could be assertive and ask the technician to explain what service was done to her car and why it was done. She is expressing her need to understand where her money is going and how her car has been repaired.

Sometimes this is the point where you begin to clarify why there is a conflict to begin with. When someone attempts to influence you, it can be at the expense of your own needs or limits. If you meet the other person's needs without addressing your own, there is still conflict, but it stays inside you. For a conflict to be completely resolved, your needs, as well as the other person's, must be affirmed. **The third step is to assert your own needs.**

PERSONAL LIFE MANAGEMENT SKILL #3
ASSERT YOUR NEEDS

Return to Assessment Activity #3 where you listed examples of evasion as a response to conflict. For those situations that you were a part of, write an assertive statement of your needs as they relate to the conflict.

Conflict Situation #1:

Assertive Needs Statement:

Conflict Situation #2:

Assertive Needs Statement:

Conflict Situation #3:

Assertive Needs Statement:

Sometimes we are surprised that other people's needs are different from our own. We get so stuck in our own brand of thinking that we forget that many other views can exist on any given subject. So, when others come up with differences, it then becomes necessary for each to begin the negotiation process.

In a successful negotiation both parties state their needs and the values they place on those individual needs. Thus, each negotiator understands the other person's viewpoint and the reasons the other person feels so strongly about that viewpoint. The truth is that it serves your own needs to understand the other person's position so that a resolution is equally supported by both parties. **Acknowledge the other person's right to have opposing needs.**

PERSONAL LIFE MANAGEMENT SKILL #4
ACKNOWLEDGE OTHERS' NEEDS

Recall a conflict that you have been involved in recently. Write below, in as much detail as you can remember, the other person's needs that related to the conflict. (Note: Since not everyone is good at expressing needs, you may have to guess what the person's needs really are. This is a common difficulty in conflict resolution.)

Conflict Situation:

Person's needs (expressed):

Person's needs (guessed):

Though there are no concrete rules of the game of conflict, like there would be rules for a board or card game, there are guidelines for communicating which can help the whole process go more smoothly. When discussing conflict, focus on the situation as the topic to be resolved. Using the "I feel" statement is a big key here. You would say, "I feel . . . (insert emotion) . . . when you . . . (insert the problem or issue)." This way of communicating ensures a discussion related to the issues, rather than an individual, emotional response to the character of the person.

It is easy to get lost in emotion in a conflict to the extent that emotion becomes your entire focus. Feelings, however, are not the issue. Behavior is the issue. By using the "I feel . . . " statements, you begin to separate the emotions from the issues. When there is intense emotion, it might be appropriate to ask yourself, "Why am I this upset about this situation?" or "Why might this other person be this upset about the situation?"

Sometimes we bring old baggage from previous, unresolved conflicts to the discussion. This baggage could be in the form of anger or hurt left over from an earlier, and maybe even unrelated, situation. If this is the case, then it is even more important to separate this excess emotion from the issues at hand. **Focus on the issues rather than the person.**

PERSONAL LIFE MANAGEMENT SKILL #5
FOCUS ON ISSUES

Think about a conflict in which you truly dislike the other person involved. Now, make a conscious effort and write down the issues of the conflict rather than the emotional effect the person has on you.

Conflict:

Person:

Issues:

(It isn't easy, is it? We have great difficulty separating our view of people from the conflict resolution business that we have with them.)

Good conflict resolution requires time and persistence. There are quick solutions to most problems, and they are arrived at fairly easily. However, these solutions are rarely the best for either party and are seldom supported for any period of time. They are often only temporary Band-Aids on a situation that requires major care. Sometimes you just have to ask the question, "What will it take for you to be satisfied in this situation?" Surprisingly, the answer is often simpler than you think.

What Do You Think?

Sasha and her husband, Michael, have just had their tenth discussion, or rather argument, about the one sore spot in their marriage: Michael wants to have a baby and Sasha does not. Michael has stormed out of the house, and Sasha has locked herself in the bathroom. Sasha has a career position with a senior management track at her company. Women who have children never seem to go anywhere in the company. There doesn't seem to be actual discrimination. It's more that those women don't stay late or come in on weekends like others on the management team do. Michael came from a very happy family with three children and feels the reason he and Sasha got married was to eventually have a family.

What emotion(s) do you think Michael is feeling?

What might Sasha be thinking?

What are the issues in this conflict?

What are Sasha's needs?

What are Michael's needs?

What might be a mutually acceptable solution to this problem?

Your goal in conflict resolution is not to make the conflict go away, but to resolve the issues that created the conflict, once and for all. As long as the issue is still a problem for the other person, it will continue to come up over and over and be a problem for you. Therefore, a mutual solution is the only workable option. **Persist in finding a solution to a mutual problem.**

PERSONAL LIFE MANAGEMENT SKILL #6
FIND MUTUAL SOLUTIONS

Select a conflict that is troublesome to you now. Write below the ideal solution for you.

Conflict description:

Ideal solution:

Now, write down what problems may persist for you if this conflict is not resolved.

Problems for you:

Problems for the other person(s):

Come up with at least five possible solutions, at least one of which must be desirable to the other person.

1.

2.

3.

4.

5.

Now, reach a mutually agreeable solution to the conflict.

Resolution:

Conflict resolution is a healthy way of solving problems when our needs differ. There will always be alternative ways of looking at any issue and alternative values placed on these issues. **Conflict is not detrimental unless we let it cripple our relationships and damage our sense of self.** Following good conflict management guidelines can ensure positive results.

PERSONAL LIFE MANAGEMENT PLAN STEP #7

Back Off and Handle Your Own Emotions

Listen with Great Attention To Detail

Assert Your Own Needs

Acknowledge the Other Person's Needs

Focus on the Issues Rather than the Person

Persist in Resolving a Mutual Problem

UNIT III PROGRESS CHECK AND AFFIRMATION

Dear Reader:

Now that you are at the end of Unit III, you have learned positive approaches to self-talk, to worry, and to conflict. You have gained control of your time so that you can begin to carry out the goals you set for yourself in Unit I. Critical thinking and creative problem solving are helping you eliminate many of the difficulties that have been standing in the way of your goal activities.

By now, with practice, you are using these new skills on a daily basis. You are also beginning to get a glimpse of your own power in being able to bring about the changes you desire.

What you are doing takes courage and persistence. Now, say to yourself, "I am effective and capable of steering my life in positive directions. I am proud of my progress. I like myself and my new operating style."

Congratulations! We are proud of you too.

Sincerely,

B.W. and S. Mc.

STAGE FOUR: BUILD EFFECTIVE RELATIONSHIPS

8 Self-Nurturing

"Take care of yourself!" we say to our friends. We enthusiastically and sincerely wish this for others, but we all too often neglect to do this for ourselves.

Taking care of ourselves is a responsibility that we cannot give away or neglect. Self-nurturing is not a luxury; it is a necessity for a mentally and emotionally fit life. Ironically, many of us grow up with the mistaken idea that someone else should take care of us. As children, we were, of course, taken care of by our parents. There comes a time, however, when it becomes necessary to take over for ourselves.

For most of us, though, there is no clear-cut time when the controls are handed over formally and we take responsibility for creating our own happiness. In high school, we take courses and progress toward a formal graduation. This graduation is a transition to a new level of education or work. But in life, there is no "graduation" from being cared for in the sense that a parent cares for a child.

As a parent myself, I can clearly see that there are still times when I want to take care of the young adults that I have lovingly looked after since birth. It is hard for parents to stop parenting. Further, I think it is sometimes even harder for the child in each of us to resist the urge to expect others to pick up where our parents left off.

The case of Jean and Tina illustrates this. As soon as Jean graduated and began to work, she moved out of her parents' house and in with her childhood friend Tina. Tina was attentive and seemed to take responsibility for Jean in many ways: cooking, sharing the names of her social contacts, and showing a real interest in Jean's beginning career. Jean felt loved and cared for, just as she had while growing up.

Eventually, though, Tina's career and social life took off, filling her evenings with work or outings with other friends. With her "caretaker" not around all the time Jean felt lonely. She eventually grew angry and criticized Tina for not "caring."

Finally, tired of the constant criticism, Tina asked Jean why she did not go out with friends or find interests of her own. Jean felt shocked and rejected. After thinking about the situation, though, she did not really know why she resisted cultivating a social life of her own. She just thought Tina was selfish and didn't care about their friendship anymore.

What is illustrated here is a difference in maturity and ability to self-nurture. Tina had learned to meet her social and professional needs through her friends and business acquaintances, in other words, to self-nurture. Jean's expectations, on the other hand, were self-centered and dependent. This behavior pattern prevented her from being creative in taking care of herself and kept her dependent on someone else for her happiness.

What Jean and others often don't realize is **there must be a time when we drop the expectations that others will do our work for us—the work of seeing to our well-being.** We must begin to act with a sense of empowerment and maturity and learn effective ways to care for ourselves. However difficult this may seem at first, it is an important step toward happiness.

It is not just the very young who experience this confusion and find it unsettling to deal with. Andy, age 42, a retired police officer on disability, came to me talking of being depressed and lonely. Andy's depression seemed to be unexplainable because his wife of 22 years, Beverly, a real estate agent, appeared to be a loving and warm person. However, it came out that Andy's feelings of isolation stemmed from his wife's often being gone in the evenings showing property.

Instead of directing his anger at Beverly, Andy turned it inward. He resented her not being around in the evenings to be supportive of and interested in him. Since he could not get her to "take care of" him, he became depressed.

Assessment Activity #1

Sometimes we get angry at people we are close to when they don't take care of us the way we think they should. Think back to the last few times you felt resentment toward a friend or family member. What do you think that person should be doing for you that he or she is not doing?

1. I think that____________________ should be____________________

   ____.

2. I think that____________________ should be____________________

   ____.

3. I think that______________________ should be__________________
____.

Andy had placed the burden of his emotional well-being on his wife. He expected her to provide a certain amount of management of his time and activities. Eventually, he began to see that this was not only unrealistic, it was unnecessary. Andy accepted that entertaining him was not his wife's job, and that he should venture into areas of self-nurturing that he enjoyed.

The plan he worked out for himself involved activities related to his previous law enforcement job. He volunteered for a commission to study gang violence in his city and eventually was hired as a consultant to set up a gang relations team. His depression began to lift, and Beverly reported after several months that their evenings together had become delightful exchanges of, "What's new with you?"

Once he took control over his own situation, and found something in which he had a sense of purpose and fulfillment, he began to realize that he could be responsible for his own happiness. He could then enjoy his wife's contribution to the marriage because he didn't expect her to meet all his emotional needs. He could take care of some of those needs himself.

Andy has demonstrated here that **each of us can change our unrealistic expectations of others.** By doing this, he took control of his unhappiness in an effective way and relieved the tension in his relationship. For those of us who struggle with unmet needs, it becomes important to look at whether expectations are realistic. Additionally, it is important for us to look for more creative ways to take care of ourselves.

Some specific ways you can take care of yourself include:

1. Recognizing and meeting your body's basic needs—rest, nutrition, exercise
2. Taking a break when needed—satisfying interests and hobbies
3. Challenging yourself to new levels of intellectual and emotional growth.

You must also take care of your needs for:

4. Privacy
5. Responsible action with finances
6. Meaningful affiliations and relationships.

Anything you do for yourself that produces a sense of well-being and serenity is self-nurturing.

What Do You Think?

David is a single parent and works on a loading dock for a parcels company. A diligent worker, he often skips lunch and also puts in extra hours to make sure the job is done right. Then he rushes home to take the kids to gymnastics and ball games. When there is no evening activity, he cooks a hot meal for the family and helps the kids with homework. Lately, he has been having trouble with panic attacks. His operating style has been high anxiety for so long, he doesn't even recognize that he is experiencing stress overload.

David has several self-nurturing needs he is not meeting. What are they?

What could David do for self-nurturing?

BODY NEEDS

The way you feel at any moment during the day can be affected by how much sleep you have gotten, what you ate for lunch, and whether you sit at a desk or move around a lot. Imbalances in the systems in your body cause changes in your nervous system and your moods.

Long-term sleep deprivation causes confusion and inability to think rationally. It is a technique commonly used by those who want to brainwash their subjects. Lowered levels of magnesium can lead to irritability as can the absence of B vitamins in the system. People who diet frequently or who exercise in hot climates notice a midday weakness caused by the loss of potassium and other body salts in sweat.

Finally, in addition to recognizing the effects of those conditions above, you need exercise on a regular basis. Exercise produces chemicals in the body that create a sense of calm— a sort of "all's right with the world" feeling. Sleeping enough, eating balanced meals, and exercising can improve the way you feel. Thus, a first step in self-nurturing is taking care of your body.

PERSONAL LIFE MANAGEMENT SKILL #1
TAKE CARE OF YOUR BODY'S NEEDS

Below, list specific things you can do to take care of your body's needs in each of the categories given. Be sure to list things you can, and will realistically, do.

1. Rest

2. Diet/nutrition

3. Exercise

BREAKS Learning when to take a break is another necessary step and is often a difficult one. Tuning in to signals your body sends you will let you see when it is time to take a break from the routine. These signals will vary with individuals but are most often: inabilty to think clearly, anger too easily aroused, stiffness in muscles, general "shaky" or queasy feeling, tiredness, and difficulty in sleeping.

A break can consist of anything from a 15-minute coffee break to a vacation at a resort. One client I have even views cleaning a horse's stall as a break from the demands of job and parenting. Many people view a hobby as an investment in relaxation and a satisfying break in the grind. A hobby can free the mind from the constant bombardment of the rigors of daily life. Whether it takes the form of a five-minute walk in the sunshine or a new interest in building model airplanes, the second step, taking a break, is an essential, nurturing activity.

PERSONAL LIFE MANAGEMENT SKILL #2
TAKE A BREAK

Below list five things you like or would like to do that might qualify as a good, nurturing break. Remember, you can include things that you do not do now, but think you would like to do.

1.

2.

3.

4.

5.

Now, go back over the list and write an approximate time needed for the activity.

Next, beside each, put 2 stars (**) for those activites that require more than one person. Remember to be open-minded about the need for others here. For example, it is possible to go to the movies alone, though you may think of that activity, at first, of requiring others.

Finally, for each, put dollar signs ($) beside those that would cost money to do. You can put 2 dollar signs ($$) beside the expensive ones like vacations or hang gliding or whatever your idea is.

You have now written your prescription for break times. Hopefully, you had some short-time and long-time activities; some people activities, and some alone; some elaborate and some economical activities. Whatever you have listed is a start toward making break times a priority for your self-nurturing.

GROWTH As you progress in your self-nurturing with body awareness and breaks in routine, another area you should be attending to is mental and emotional growth. In business, companies that do not grow often go into decline. People are much the same; nourishing mental and emotional thoughts and activities become essential to self-nurturing. Growth enriches us.

The book you are reading right now is an example of your steps to grow mentally and emotionally. It challenges you to consider new ideas and new ways of behaving that will add to your happiness. You will find, however, that as you add to your knowledge, you will begin to want more. This third step is the sign of a healthy person— to see self-awareness and growth in understanding as an adventure, not as a threat.

PERSONAL LIFE MANAGEMENT SKILL #3
CHALLENGE FOR GROWTH

For growth you must go outside the knowledge that is part of your daily life. This is the role of curiosity. Below, list ideas you are curious about in each of the areas designated. An example might be related to something you have wondered about: "How did successful people get that way?" or "Why does lightning strike one place more often than another?"

Area one. Think of two processes, related to your work, that you could learn more about. At the same time write down where you might go to get the information.

1. Process one:

2. Process two:

Area two. Think about two people you know who seem really "together" most of the time. What questions could you ask them to help you to understand how they operate that makes them so adept at managing their lives?

Question #1:

Question #2:

Area three. Pick up a guide from a local community school that offers special interest, adult courses. These range from wine tasting and canoeing to investments and business writing. Choose two subject areas you would be interested in pursuing either by taking the course or by reading about the subject.

Subject Area #1:

Subject Area #2:

PRIVACY As we look at body awareness, routine breaks, and mental growth, we have to keep in mind that sometimes we have the need to just be alone with ourselves and our thoughts. *Privacy,* a word that reflects an important need for all of us , is simply the need for time alone. The act itself sets up a sense of having a boundary that others must not cross. It reflects our ability to set limits on unhealthy intrusions from our surroundings. It gives us a space where we can re-group, reflect, and refresh our sense of who we are.

Yet, for some, private time alone is a frightening prospect. It gets misinterpreted as feelings of loneliness and emptiness. For many, it feels like isolation, and the isolation brings on more tension and stress.

But the truth here is that private time alone is a requirement for self-nurturing. Without it we lose ourselves in the demands of the world; we diminish our capacity for self-knowledge. By avoiding these private times, we restrict our capacity for self-growth. In essence, **privacy is both a state of being and a purposeful act of replenishing the elements of our personal identity.** In the fourth step, by choosing privacy, we empower ourselves to think and grow.

PERSONAL LIFE MANAGEMENT SKILL #4
CREATE PRIVACY

For this activity you should be in a quiet place, or at least a place where you are not likely to be interrupted.

1. Close your eyes and take a moment to picture a place where you feel secure and protected. (For some it is a memory of a childhood treehouse, for you, it might be a creek bank or your favorite chair at home.)

2. Try to recall the good feelings you have had there and allow yourself to enjoy them. You can be comfortable with being alone in your secure place.
3. Now, pick three places that you can go to find privacy in your daily surroundings.

   (Note: If you feel like you have no quiet places in your life right now, libraries, empty meeting rooms, and churches can provide the right environment.)

   1.

   2.

   3.

4. Plan to spend some time with just yourself this week. If you begin to feel uncomfortable being alone in the place you have picked, just recall the place you described earlier. At first, try a few minutes sitting or resting quietly and thinking about some of the ideas you have learned in this book.
5. Lengthen the time you spend thinking by yourself over a week until you are comfortable spending more and more time becoming enriched with the self-discovery process.

FINANCES

The underpinning of financial management, though sometimes a tedious detail in our lives, is security. Without the security of finances that meet your obligations, you will have difficulty focusing on other important aspects of your life. A brief analysis of your current status will suggest the directions you need to go to get the money aspect of your life to a more comfortable place.

Sometimes, just deciding which of your expenditures falls into the category of "essential" and which would be "desirable," is the starting point. For example, having a few mix-and-match pieces of clothing that could be useful for casual or work wear would be "essential." Having a complete wardrobe for each—work and casual—would be "desirable." Most overspending seems to fall into the category of those things we feel are desirable.

It is always difficult to look at finances objectively because we sometimes define ourselves by the things that we buy. "Boy, in that suit I'll look just like the V.P.s" or "I know that car is more than my budget, but it's really me." We have our trademark cologne, nightclubs, and clothes. **Separating our sense of self from those things we surround ourselves with will help keep our spending under control.**

Finally, just keeping track of finances, some sort of record-keeping system, assures us that we are financially secure and that we are taking care of ourselves. The key to proper financial management is understanding that it can reduce our stress and pave the way for our moving into more meaningful pursuits. In Skill #5 **we balance our need for things with clear and realistic plans for ensuring our financial well-being.**

PERSONAL LIFE MANAGEMENT SKILL #5
MANAGE FINANCES RESPONSIBLY

Make a list below of things you would like to purchase in the near future. Identify whether each fits the category of "essential" or "desirable."

	ESSENTIAL	DESIRABLE
1.		
2.		
3.		
4.		
5.		
6.		

Now, put those items you labeled as "desirable" into a priority list. Number them in order of your need to purchase them. (Note: If all on your list are "essential," then you might need to look at them again. You need occasional unnecessary treats, but if all purchases seem essential, you may be attaching undue value to some things.)

AFFILIATIONS

As we mature and begin to accept responsibility for our own care in many areas, we must also recognize our need to be affiliated with people we enjoy. This begins with the family, which is the first meaningful affiliation we are involved in. As adults, we have a natural instinct to continue being involved with others. These relationships are with people who have similar values or interests. Although the type of affiliations we had as children will change as we mature, the expectations from these associations remain similar in nature. What most people want is:

1. A sense of belonging
2. A sense of self-esteem
3. A sense of being valued and appreciated
4. A sense of accomplishment

Some specific types of affiliations are: friendship, acquaintances, church groups, social or civic clubs, charitable organizations, professional organizations, educational institutions, and work settings. For example, many workers rate recognition for a job well done higher than job security or pay in what they value in the workplace. Churches are formed because people of the same religious beliefs want to congregate. Civic groups grow out of mutual need for camaraderie and service.

Finding out we are not alone in our beliefs or likes or needs is reassuring for most of us. Very bright children often feel hopelessly out of place until they move to an educational setting with other equally bright children. If you are a racing fan, going to a car race will lead you to others who share your enthusiasm. Affiliations, in a way, become our extended family and provide nurturing in many different facets of our lives. Skill #6, forming meaningful affililations, is a way of nurturing ourselves by belonging to groups with which we share common interests.

PERSONAL LIFE MANAGEMENT SKILL #6
FORM MEANINGFUL AFFILIATIONS

Below, name several groups you are presently affiliated with. Identify whether the affiliation is meaningful or not based on the guidelines above.

1.

2.

3.

4.

Now, name three (3) groups you feel a desire to be affiliated with that would increase your abililty to self-nurture.

1.

2.

3.

Identify one change you will now commit to regarding affiliations.

Change:

LIMITS Caution must be observed here. As you begin looking for ways to take care of yourself, remember that activity that increases stress or becomes destructive to self or others is not nurturing. It is possible to overdo.

To see this even more clearly look at the following example:

> You are hungry and haven't eaten all afternoon. When you finally do sit down to a meal, you eat everything in sight. You have satisfied your appetite , but feel guilty for overeating, and probably have a great deal of physical discomfort from it as well. The attempt at nurture on one level has taken on a negative end result: the outcome of the behavior has become self-defeating rather than nurturing.

Balance is important in maintaining emotional fitness. Excesses of anything: work, food, spending, even exercise, can destroy balance. Then the activity is no longer nurturing.

As you begin examining your life at work or at home, your involvement with others must also be examined. Self-nurturing should not be completely at the expense of those with whom you live or work. That becomes selfishness, another self-defeating action. Imagine what would happen if we only focused on ourselves, regardless of what others' needs were. Self-nurturing would then be perceived by others as self-centered behavior and would thus create ill feelings in relationships.

PERSONAL LIFE MANAGEMENT SKILL #7
OBSERVE LIMITS

Now, look at the nurturing activities you have written in Skill #3 above and see if you can identify a point at which any of these activities could become self-defeating.

1. I plan to ________________________, but it could be self-defeating if ____.

2. I plan to ________________________, but it could be self-defeating if ____.

3. I plan to ________________________, but it could be self-defeating if ____.

Once you accept the responsibility for your own nurture, you will find yourself less vulnerable to outside influences. Relieving others of the responsibility for your care and happiness will ultimately bring a feeling of security and serenity. In taking control of your own nurturing, you reduce your reliance on others and the anger you might have from unfulfilled expectations. By making self-nurture a part of your life plan, you ensure a capacity for more satisfying relationships and a greater potential for personal well-being.

PERSONAL LIFE MANAGEMENT STEP #8

Recognize and Care for Body Needs

Take aBreak when Needed

Challenge Yourself for Growth

Create Positive Privacy

Manage Finances Responsibly

Form Meaningful Affiliations

Developing Sustaining Relationships

In the last chapter you began to learn the importance of self-nurturing, of recognizing and taking care of needs you have. Sustaining relationships extend the concept of self-nurturing. They provide a richness that we simply cannot afford to live without. In actuality, I believe that these relationships become cushions that buffer our spirits from adversity. This is not to say that they take away or protect us from all trouble, but they do shore us up at times and help us to maintain balance.

These relationships also act as mirrors and let us know what we are presenting to the world. Finding and maintaining these relationships is not always easy. I would venture to guess that a large portion of the people I see in my practice have few close affiliations outside of family, and some don't even have good ones there. Instead of being sustaining, these relationships are draining.

Draining Relationships

A case I have seen recently points up this issue. Anna is an attorney, married to a successful building contractor, and has one child. She originally came to me with her husband for marriage counseling. Eventually, it came out that one of the problems with the marriage was Anna's brother, Scott, who had been living with Anna and her husband since he had been laid off from his job as an electronics installer.

Anna feels like she is responsible for Scott, since their parents are no longer living. Scott contributes nothing to the household expenses or maintenance. Anna's husband doesn't mind the financial expense of Scott's living there, but he does resent the additional burden placed on Anna. He thinks Scott should at least help out around the house and look for a new job. Anna feels sorry for Scott because he has been depressed over the unexpected layoff.

At a therapy session we find out that Anna feels powerless to handle

Scott and has been irritable with the rest of the family because of it. What has happened is that Scott has taken advantage of his sister and brother-in-law's hospitality. The situation has been draining Anna because she has a number of mixed feelings about her brother.

Often we are involved with people that we like, but they take advantage of us in some way. Not only do they drain us with their constant needs, they cause intense frustration because we don't know how to make them stop. These are not sustaining relationships, no matter how much loyalty and affection the person involved professes and no matter how much you like the person otherwise. The other person must be concerned with your needs in a balanced way, not just with your ability to satisfy his or her needs, in order for the relationship to be sustaining.

When Anna realized what was really going on, she was able to do some constructive problem solving and discuss the situation with her brother in a positive way. After their discussion Scott became more aware and supportive of his sister's needs. He began to do more around the house, and discussed with the family the possibility of his going back to finish school.

Scott and Anna did not have a sustaining relationship because neither really understood what the other person needed. In addition, there was no apparent communication about feelings. Anna's frustration at being unable to deal with Scott led to her irritability with her family.

Many draining relationships have certain aspects in common:

1. Consistent frustration with the way the relationship goes
2. Lack of trust and open communication about feelings
3. Guarded feeling as if a threat is present but unidentifiable
4. Few positive exchanges of needs
5. The feeling that something "just isn't right"

Sometimes relationships that drain are hard to identify. Since relationships evolve, it is possible for the situation to start out as sustaining, but one or the other of you may begin to sap the emotional strength from the relationship.

Ways people drain others in relationships include: being argumentative, being too agreeable, wanting things their way all the time, imposing on time or privacy, manipulating, and being "too needy" all the time. For example, if a good friend consistently shows up at your house unannounced and expects your time and attention, that friend is draining. Friends who call constantly to talk about problems with everyone from their boss to the clerk at the store can make you feel almost physically tired after the conversations.

The "dump and run" type drops a problem in your lap, expecting you to provide solutions. When this friend leaves, you feel weighed down from all the other person's problems. Employees who spend part of every day in the manager's office over problems with their jobs are draining.

Assessment Activity #1

After looking at the above descriptions and examples, write below some present or past relationships that have been draining for you and describe how they are draining.

1. Name:

   This person(s) drains me in the following way:

2. Name:

   This person(s) drains me in the following way:

3. Name:

   This person (s) drains me in the following way:

SUSTAINING RELATIONSHIPS

Sustaining relationships contribute to our overall well-being and sense of being valued and cared for. There are different ways this is demonstrated according to the type of relationship involved. But sustaining relationships have certain characteristics in common:

1. Comfort and consistency allow free emotions, laughter, or tears.
2. Both persons and their feelings are valued.
3. Needs are met in a reciprocal fashion.
4. Listening is two-way and responsive.
5. Personal limits and boundaries are respected (time and space).

From a sustaining relationship we draw strength of spirit. These associations have reasonable expectations and provide reasonable support. As discussed in the self-nurturing chapter, relationships should not have to be our only source of nurture. But, they are important for affirming us as individuals who have value.

What Do You Think?

A college student, Leonard, was taking a course with his major professor. This professor had encouraged Leonard through the trials of his freshman year and had shown a real interest in Leonard's success. Leonard went to this professor for mentoring when he was trying to choose a major. Throughout his college time he has felt generally supported by this man whom he has grown to respect a great deal. So, when he received a "D" on a paper from this teacher, he was not only upset at the grade, but he felt embarrassed to have scored so low for this person. In addition, his feelings were hurt that his "friend" could have given him such a low grade.

What could Leonard say to his professor to confront the situation and still preserve the relationship?

How should the professor respond to be supportive of Leonard?

Our sustaining relationships are people we can, and often do, laugh with; not just polite snickers, but the kind of guffaws saved for only those special times among our closest friends and relatives. This laughter has tremendous therapeutic effect, which is one of the reasons it is such an important nurturing element.

When we laugh, the brain causes endorphins to be released. These hormones are the body's natural tranquilizers. They help to counter the damaging effects of stress. Thus, the more we laugh, the healthier we become.

Other ways people contribute to good relationships include: showing courtesy and respect, listening to ideas even when they differ, showing interest in your needs, displaying interest in maintaining the relationship, accepting mistakes without criticizing, encouraging you when you need hope.

On the job, two people may have conflicting views about how a problem should be solved. People in a sustaining relationship will respect each others' views and work to arrive at a mutually acceptable solution. Sustainers will make it a point to wish you well the day of your scheduled job interview. "Hand holding" sustainers will always provide a "port in the storm" in case of crisis.

Assessment Activity #2

After looking at the above descriptions of sustaining relationships, write down people with whom you have this kind of relationship and the way they sustain you.

1. Name:

   This person(s) sustains me in the following ways:

2. Name:

   This person(s) sustains me in the following ways:

3. Name:

   This person(s) sustains me in the following ways:

Just for discussion's sake, in any of the above situations that you noted as sustaining, is there the potential that they could evolve into draining relationships? For a moment, you might consider the roles each of you plays in the sustaining of the relationship and look for areas you might choose to improve.

BUILDING BETTER RELATIONSHIPS

Now that you have looked at your relationships, past and present, to decide whether they are draining or sustaining, you are ready to move to the next stage. This will be your work in building better relationships: turning around or abandoning draining ones, and enhancing and strengthening sustaining ones.

Several skills are involved in building relationships that are satisfying and nurturing. The term *building* is a correct description of what you will be doing because solid, sustaining relationships do not happen without care and attention.

One essential requirement for this process is learning to understand the needs of others and to realize and assert your own needs within the relationship. Understandably, the boundaries of these needs will have to be adjusted depending on the nature of the association. For instance, families often meet certain needs for each other without even having to be asked. But, in the workplace, you might have to assert your needs for privacy, or for training, or for a raise, and let these be known in specific, perhaps written, ways to receive the support you need.

SUPPORTIVE LISTENING

One way to learn where another person's need is "coming from" is with supportive listening. This is an attentive, nonjudgmental activity where you invite one another to express needs in a clear-cut fashion. Obviously, this is a helpful activity only if there is a sincere desire to understand one another's wants and wishes where the relationship is concerned. Below is an example of supportive listening:

Glenn: I am so frustrated with my job. I can't stand this place anymore. I'm just about ready to quit.

Janice: You seem really upset. Can you tell me exactly what is disturbing you?

Glenn: We are having constant problems with materials arriving on time so we can complete our work orders. Those purchasing people just don't care about us!

Janice: This sounds like something you really need to get resolved. Let's see how we can look at this to solve the problem.

In this exchange, Janice is not taking on Glenn's problem, but she is acknowledging that Glenn feels strongly about what is happening. This supports Glenn because she has taken him seriously. She has helped Glenn look at what he is feeling and has offered to engage in problem-solving activity with him.

PERSONAL LIFE MANAGEMENT SKILL #1
USE SUPPORTIVE LISTENING

Seek out a friend or family member that you sense is experiencing a problem of some sort. Get him or her to share it with you. Your instructions are to respond to that person's statements, not by offering solutions, but by saying supportive things as in the conversation above.

Example: "My wife has been so hard to live with since the baby was born. I almost hate to go home in the evenings anymore."

Supportive response: It sounds like the situation is really getting to you.

"I just don't know what to do anymore."

Supportive response: Is there anything I can do to help you solve this problem?

Situation #1:

Problem statement:

Supportive response:

Situation #2:

Problem statement:

Supportive response:

In addition to listening to other people's needs in a sustaining relationship, you must be able to voice your own needs. Sometimes this requires assertiveness; sometimes it's just understanding what you want and being able to say it.

VOICING NEEDS

You must be able to talk about what you want from relationships in a positive way. Some find it difficult to really ask for attention, support, or even affection. It is important to say what you need so that the other person in the relationship has an opportunity to at least understand what you want. The following exchange shows this:

Elaine: Every time I come to your house our conversations are constantly being interrupted by the telephone ringing. By the time I leave, I feel frustrated because I can't get more than a sentence out without an interruption.

Robin: I didn't know it bothered you so much.

Elaine can tell Robin how she feels without being insulting or critical. By voicing her feelings, she has given Robin a chance to respond and to deal with the situation. Had Elaine, instead, not said anything, she might just have become more and more angry and begun visiting less.

PERSONAL LIFE MANAGEMENT SKILL #2
VOICE NEEDS

1. Find a friend who is a good listener or use a tape recorder
2. Begin talking about what your needs are
3. Practice distinguishing between wants and needs
4. Make each statement reflective of yourself rather than focusing on another person

   I feel a desire/need for ______________________ in my life.

   I feel a desire/need for ______________________ in my life.

   I feel a desire/need for ______________________ in my life.

HANDLING CONFLICTING NEEDS

As you grow more comfortable with voicing and listening to needs, conflicting needs will naturally arise. Because we are not clones of each other, we have differing views, sometimes, of what is important. These conflicts help us learn more about each other.

When these occasions occur, these conflicts must be addressed immediately so that frustration does not build up. A child often has a need to play rather than do assigned chores around the house. Parents feel strongly about children doing assigned chores. This conflict of needs can escalate quickly into a power struggle if not handled correctly. Using conflict-management and problem-solving skills, the parents and child can arrive at a solution suitable to both and consistent with the values of both.

When conflicts occur, you can use the skills you learned in Chapter 6 on conflict management. **Caring confrontation and resolution of conflicts is necessary to sustaining relationships.** Look at the following exchange between Elaine and Robin, who were introduced earlier.

Elaine: Yes, the phone does bother me. I come over to talk to my friend, not to listen to you talk to others on the phone while I sit here.

At this point Elaine has voiced a need. Robin, to be supportive, must address Elaine's statement in a caring way.

Robin: I understand your feelings, but you know I have a catering business, and my customers can only reach me here during the day. To run a business, I have to spend a certain amount of time on the phone.

So, the need conflict surfaces in what could be a potential problem in the relationship between the two friends. Elaine, having heard Robin's need statement, should also use supportive communication and go to a problem-solving mode.

Elaine: This does sound like we both have a problem. Can we look at possible solutions?

Now, the solution is not as important as the fact that the two friends are making genuine efforts to create a workable alternative to the situation that is troubling their relationship.

PERSONAL LIFE MANAGEMENT SKILL #3
HANDLE CONFLICTING NEEDS

1. Call to mind several important relationships where there are conflicting needs.
2. Try and think of options on both sides of the situation that would contribute to the solution. Try to leave out your emotions. Just let the reasoning part of your personality come up with solutions that could be workable.

   I am having a conflicting need with ___________________.

   The conflicting needs are

   ____.

The following are options we can look at which will move us to a solution:

A.

B.

C.

D.

E.

One difficulty that enters into relationship conflicts, and in some cases actually contributes to need conflicts, is the fear of rejection. This fear may be the result of excess baggage brought into adulthood from a non-nurturing, negative childhood. Children who feel as if their parents didn't really care for them grow up to be adults who worry that the ones they love won't love them back.

In the case of Elaine and Robin, Elaine felt rejected by Robin's constant telephone conversations with others. Robin did not see the situation this way at all. She was just running her business. Actually, Elaine could have been more respectful of Robin's needs to talk with customers. For this example a good solution might be scheduled visits when Robin's not so tied up.

RE-THINKING REJECTION

Everyone has fears of rejection. **The truth is, not everyone has to like you for you to have satisfying relationships.** Work acquaintances don't necessarily have to become your best friends, nor do others with whom you have not built a relationship. Another thought is that what may seem like rejection may not actually be that at all.

The "friend" you have coffee with every day at work might have a big project due. By noting that person's need for being left alone, you can be a supportive friend instead of putting yourself in a situation that could lead to feelings of rejection.

Sometimes, though, you will come across people who just do not wish to be in a relationship with you as badly as you wish to be involved with them. This situation requires you to re-examine the definition you have of rejection. In childhood, rejection meant a loss; it created sadness. So, we take that old definition into adult life when, actually, we should re-define the concept of rejection.

If someone chooses not to have a relationship with you, this could be the result of incompatible goals, differing relationship needs, or even non-meshing life schedules—some people are work-oriented rather than people/relationship oriented. Other people could be so preoccupied with their own problems that they don't even think in terms of "like" or "dislike."

So, rejection becomes a dropping back to the level where you were dependent on others for your nurture. Remembering the self-nurturing skills you have already learned will help you take a more rational view of the effect of others including you in their relationships or not.

PERSONAL LIFE MANAGEMENT SKILL #4
RE-THINK REJECTION

1. Think of the last time you felt rejected.
2. Describe the scene in which the perceived rejection occurred.
3. Does this remind you of a situation from the past, and could the past experience color how you view this situation?
4. Do you think the other person had some other life incident going on that could have been distracting ?
5. How can you apply adult reasoning to the situation so that you can replace hurt with understanding?

The situation was:

____.

What could have been going on with me was:

____.

What could have been going on with the other person was:

____.

How can you adjust your view of the situation to make it positive for you? __________________________________.

(Now use this format to work through other times when you felt rejected.)

Sustaining relationships are those which give us a sense of belonging. They help us when we need help and they are reciprocal. They give us the opportunity to "be there" for others in a nurturing way. They are a source of new energy when we are drained by the rigors of life.

PERSONAL LIFE MANAGEMENT PLAN STEP #9

Use Supportive Listening

Voice Needs

Handle Conflicting Needs

Re-think Rejection

Cultivating Intimate Relationships

Most of us struggle with intimacy—some run from it, some pursue it with the same energy. Many do not know what intimacy is and are afraid to ask. This confusion is understandable, since there are no clear-cut guidelines for us to follow to develop intimate relationships. Consequently, many of us remain confused in our efforts to create these. The following story is a perfect example of this confusion.

Monica and Eddie were referred to me by the divorce court for pre-divorce arbitration. Their first visit was set up by Monica in an effort to help Eddie realize why she wanted to divorce him. He hadn't the first clue as to what the problem was and why she was leaving him. Said Eddie, " I don't understand it. I bought her a nice house. She doesn't have to work, I've seen to that. I have never treated her badly. I don't think we ever even had a fight until this."

Monica's version sounded much different, "Living with Eddie was like having a roommate. He came home at night, sure. But he would rather be at the office or out in his shop doing anything but talking with me. He never wanted to hear what I had to say about my feelings. He just shut me out."

Why did Eddie and Monica have such different views of the same situation? The answer is that for each of them intimacy (which in their case meant marriage) had very different meanings. For Monica, marriage meant physical and emotional closeness and support. For Eddie, it meant working hard to give Monica "gifts" in the form of house and such. This was supposed to provide her with happiness. Instead, his constant preoccupation with working and his hobbies caused her pain and loneliness.

So, the question must be raised, what is intimacy? A definition from a dictionary is far too inadequate to describe something as complex as intimate relationships. But, a look at what intimate associations are not, compared with what they are, may lead us to a few guidelines on what to look for. After that, it may be helpful to learn how to assess our own relationships and to develop those that we can truly call "intimate."

Assessment Activity # 1

Take a moment and write down your own view of what intimacy is. Try to describe a relationship that you think would fit your definition of the level of intimacy that would feel good to you.

My view of an intimate relationship is:

As an additional activity that might help you further clarify your view, ask a friend to write down his or her view and see how the two definitions compare.

Friend's definition:

First, let's look at what an ineffective approach to relationships might be. It will help to have some guidelines on what to avoid.

INEFFECTIVE RELATIONSHIPS

One rather well-to-do businessman I know has told me and many others about all the "close friends" he has among politically influential people. He mentions places they have all flown to on a weekend just to fish or play golf. Often he even shows pictures taken with these friends on a boat or at an exotic bar on some island.

In therapy, though, this same man confided to me that he felt an emptiness or alone-ness in his life that he couldn't understand. He said that there was no one who he really felt cared for him other than what he could do for them. His comment was especially telling:

"I am 42 years old, and I don't think I have anyone that I can call a 'real friend.'"

When I asked him what that meant, a "real friend," he responded, "I don't know exactly, but I don't feel like I have one."

He tried to create intimacy by having parties and taking people places. Even among his many "girlfriends," the relationships never seemed to last any length of time.

Intimacy is not forced or bought or contrived. It is not created with "hidden agendas." You cannot get intimacy by tricking people or making them owe you or depend on you. In the above situation, my client attempted to win friends by showing them a good time. Intimate friends are willing to share the bad times too. This is what he was missing.

The businessman mentioned above did not have a clear picture of what an intimate relationship really was. Perhaps a view of intimacy, as represented by the immensely popular TV show, *Cheers*, contributes to our lack of understanding about what real intimacy is in relationships. The characters in that show defined their relationships in a bar, not in a family, not with a special person, but with a group of folks that gathered every evening to drink. It is possible that there are many of us who are, as the song said, "Looking for love in all the wrong places." And television may be supporting the illusion that we can find intimacy in artificial situations.

If we are having difficulty with relationships and don't understand what goes wrong time after time, maybe a look at what ineffective relationships are will help. These intimacy-lacking affiliations will have:

1. Lack of communication—feelings and ideas are not exchanged freely.
2. Lack of commitment—indecision and distance prevent intimacy.
3. Unresolved anger—resentment exists from past or present hurts.
4. Conflicting goals—differences appear in what each needs and is willing to give.
5. Conflicting values—disagreement occurs over what is important.
6. Thoughtlessness—disregard emerges for the feelings of the other.
7. Irresponsibility—carelessness mishandles possessions or duties.
8. Self-centeredness—demands for self-satisfaction become constant neediness.

Even one or two of these characteristics can block growth and development in a relationship. Granted, there are very few perfect relationships. But, failure to acknowledge and deal with any of these problems can lead to the breakdown of the connection between two people.

Assessment Activity #2

Using the list of characteristics above, list relationships you either are now involved in or have been in that might be ineffective for you. Remember that there are all sorts of relationships, so be sure to look at all your closest ones.

1. Person's name:

   Type of relationship (family, friend, lover, etc.):

   This relationship is ineffective because:

2. Person's name:

   Type of relationship :

   This relationship is ineffective because:

3. Person's name:

   Type of relationship:

   This relationship is ineffective because:

(Note: It is important that you examine all your close relationships. If you run out of room in this activity, use another sheet of paper to continue.)

INTIMATE RELATIONSHIPS

Couples' relationships are not the only places where intimacy problems can occur. In many families, the very base from which most of us draw our support, there can be withheld love, distance, and coldness. Anyone who has grown up in one of these families can attest that they feel confused over what love really is. If the family, our first exposure to what love should be, does not offer that warm, intimate relationship we expect, then what does love or intimacy really look like?

It can take many forms. Some examples are: the way a coach puts a bit of himself into the development of the players on a team; the way old friends who haven't seen each other in years pick right up with conversation and sharing; and the way neighbors can sometimes step in and know what needs to be done in a crisis. All these are intimate relationships, but they all look different.

My favorite example, though, is a story a dear friend told me. His childhood remembrance of this wonderful, caring kind of relationship was the "cookie lady." He told of a neighbor at whose house he would stop to visit and who would offer him cookies. Many afternoons they would talk about what went on at school or what he dreamed about for the future, or what she had done as a child. He confessed that when he had done well on a paper at school, he would rush to show it to the "cookie lady" even before he took it to his own parents.

Maybe our intimate relationships should be with those **people who are willing to be our "fans," who will cheer for us in our attempts, and stand with us in our failures.** Below are some guidelines that will help you identify intimate relationships. You may find that you already have some that you may not have acknowledged. Look at the list below and apply it to your ideas of what intimate relationships are like.

1. Respect for each other's needs—mutual willingness to negotiate some needs for the best interests of the relationship.

2. Acceptance—both feel that weaknesses as well as strengths are understood.

3. Safety—physical and emotional trust that goes both ways.

4. Affirmation—validation and support that goes beyond tolerance.

5. Listening—value on both sides for what the other has to say.

6. Openness—ability to express guilt, anger, dreams, disappointments and know they will be handled in a kind way.

7. Closeness—physical (not necessarily sex) and emotional level of comfort comparable to your old, favorite shirt or childhood toy.

Assessment Activity # 3

Now, identify those relationships you are in that are truly intimate. Don't forget the ones that have endured over time and may be long distance.

1. Person's name:

   Type of relationship (family, lover, friend, etc.):

   This relationship is intimate because (use the describing words in the list above):

2. Person's name:

   Type of relationship:

   This relationship is intimate because:

3. Person's name:

   Type of relationship:

   This relationship is intimate because:

(Note: You may continue on another sheet of paper. You are fortunate if you have many intimate relationships, but these are rare, and many people find they only have a few. You should record and savor each in this activity.)

INCREASING INTIMACY IN RELATIONSHIPS

You need intimate relationships in your life. We all do. You can fool yourself for a little while into thinking that superficial loves are desirable. You can make yourself believe that low-key associations, the ones with no entanglements, the ones that require little energy to maintain, are the best for you. But, in truth, you need the real thing, an intimate relationship—at least in some form. Some of these will be family, some friends, some lovers, some co-workers.

People who are in intimate relationships—and this is not just the sexual, mate-for-life thing necessarily—get many benefits from them. They get a sense of calmness and security. They feel supported mentally and emotionally—someone cares about their ideas and their feelings. An intimate relationship is a place to learn more about yourself, a place to develop maturity and share dreams. Doesn't sound so bad, does it?

What Do You Think?

Given that people of different cultural backgrounds or gender communicate very differently about their feelings and needs, how can both parties in an intimate relationship be sure they understand each other?

Okay, admittedly it isn't easy. There is a lot of work involved because needs must be shared and met; talking must be paired with listening, and respect must build trust. But nothing keeps us going, keeps us alive like knowing there are folks who care for and about us. As you continue in this chapter, you will be learning how to build the kind of relationships that are satisfying at many levels, relationships that are worth the work.

There are three basic steps you need to follow:

1. Know yourself—really know who you are and what you want.
2. Follow the guide rules above for the conditions of intimacy.
3. Be persistent—practice the good behaviors that support the relationship, even if you don't feel like it at that moment.

These steps sound too simplistic, and at some level they are. But, if you understand each one thoroughly, and practice what each teaches, you can develop the kinds of relationships that truly offer you what you need.

KNOW YOURSELF

Up to this section in this book, you have been examining your life and the skills you use to manage it. You should be at a point far from where you started. In Chapter 1 you developed a vision of your desired destiny. In

Chapter 2 you uncovered the trouble spots. As you have progressed, you have learned communication and relationship skills as well as ways to make things change in your life.

Take a break to review what you have discovered in your self-examination. What really does make you the individual you are? What have you changed already that is working for you? Where do you hope to go with your life and your relationships? The answers to these questions will help you come into a relationship with a clear view of what you need and what you are prepared to offer.

PERSONAL LIFE MANAGEMENT SKILL #1
KNOW YOURSELF

Write down why you want to have an intimate relationship and what you expect from the other person. Go into as much detail as you can and be certain to explore different types of relationships you may want to have.

From a family relationship I would call intimate I need:

I am prepared to offer:

From a friend relationship I need:

I am prepared to offer:

From a lover relationship I need:

I am prepared to offer:

From other relationships I need:

I am prepared to offer:

FOLLOW THE RULES

The next step toward intimacy is to be certain you always remember the rules of intimate relationships.

Respecting each other's needs may be as simple as doing quiet activities in the late evening when the other person goes to bed early. Or it may be as complex as learning to work around a job where one of you is on call at all hours.

Accepting another's odd habits or differing beliefs does not mean you have to agree with that person. You must understand that no two people think or act exactly alike, and there are just some things that you may have to decide not to be upset about. When the other person makes clothing, career, or belief choices that are not the same as your own, you must grant that person's right to make those choices. If you do not take such choices as a personal affront, this should not be a problem.

Safety today in intimate relationships has a whole new meaning with the constant threat of AIDS (Acquired Immune Deficiency Syndrome). For sexual relationships, safety is a serious matter. Other concerns, though less profound, should be addressed also. Each person in an intimate relationship should feel that the other person will not try to inflict hurt—either physical or emotional. Each should feel that the other will use care in offering criticism that is constructive and not spiteful, that advice will be given in love and not jealousy or anger.

Affirmation should come in the form of saying, "Yes, I am with you; I believe what you are saying has value" maybe even, "I like the way you handled that argument with the kids today." Everyone needs a cheerleader, a booster. People in intimate relationships offer that boost out of genuine respect and admiration. Good things don't need to go without saying. Remember that the occasional, "I'm really proud of you" or "You look like a real winner today" should become a part of your daily conversation, not just a rare compliment.

Listening can be a high compliment, while non-listening can be a deadly insult. Have you ever been in a situation where you needed to speak to someone about something important, and the other person didn't even look up from what he or she was doing to answer you? Or the other person repeatedly looked at his or her watch? Intimacy brings with it a commitment for time and attention. What each of you has to say is important—especially in discussions about feelings. Most conflicts can be averted or resolved with careful listening.

Openness is difficult for some in a relationship. Many of my women clients report frustration in their relationships with men: "He won't tell me what he is thinking! I know he must be angry about something, but I can't get him to open up and tell me what it is."

Men, on the other hand, often complain that women get their feelings hurt "over nothing." The women neglect to tell the men what they need in the way of affection, or birthday celebrations, or special remembrances.

Openness says that you can feel free to try out a new idea or confess a secret lifelong dream and that it will be met with interest, not criticism.

Closeness just seems to happen in intimate relationships. You feel calm and relaxed in the presence of people with whom you are intimate. There is a connectedness that you may not even be able to define or describe. A sort of warmth is noticeable, and it is accompanied by a sense of peace whenever you are together. For some, the closeness is intellectual, based on ideas exchanged. For others, it may be more emotional, a lift from the sound of a voice on the phone. You can't create closeness with presents, favors, or sex. It is built out of all the other elements mentioned above.

PERSONAL LIFE MANAGEMENT SKILL #2
FOLLOW THE RULES

Make a list of rules you will follow for improving each of the relationships you are currently involved in.

Relationship #1:

Name:

Nature of relationship:

Rules for intimacy improvement:

Relationship #2:

Name:

Nature of relationship:

Rules for intimacy improvement:

Relationship #3:

Name:

Nature of relationship:

Rules for intimacy improvement:

BE PERSISTENT

The first thing to say about persistence is what it is not; it is *not* nagging someone to get them to change or to agree with you. Practice and persistence are related: practicing those behaviors that lead to intimacy over time leads to positive habits that ensure positive outcomes and good relationships. The part in this that requires care and judgment, however, is persisting in those things that enhance the relationship.

A good example for comparison is teaching. By definition, teaching does not take place unless learning also occurs. Standing in front of a class or buying educational software does not become teaching unless someone is learning from it. The same holds true with persistence in relationships.

You can give your sons or daughters gifts and money and favors in trying to show how much you love them. You can persist in this throughout their lives. But, you can miss a chance for creating a truly intimate relationship with your sons or daughters if you do not ask them what behaviors demonstrate love to them. It might be just listening to problems without dictating solutions, or it might be saying "no" sometimes when they test you on a shaky issue.

Persistence also comes in the form of pursuing conflict resolution rather than conflict suppression. An intimate relationship should have both room for conflict and motivation to resolve conflicting views or needs to the satisfaction of *both* parties, not just one or the other. As the chapter on conflict suggested, in a situation where there is disagreement, there is a *mutual* problem. Nowhere is this more true than in intimate relationships.

A chemically dependent teenager is not just a problem for her parents, she is a problem for her sister as well. Persistence in resolving conflicts so that they do not continue to come up over and over requires some dedication. The parents may get resolution by placing the teenager into a treatment center, but the sister may still be left with disturbing feelings over the whole process. Intimate relationships require persistence; intimate partners deserve it.

PERSONAL LIFE MANAGEMENT SKILL #3
BE PERSISTENT

Name two things you feel you should persist in to maintain your intimate relationships. (Note: Sometimes these are good things you already do that you feel are important for you to continue.)

Relationship #1:

1:

2:

Relationship #2:

1:

2:

Relationship #3:

1:

2:

Name two conflicts in your intimate relationships you feel have not been completely resolved. Then write what actions you will take to persist in their resolution.

Conflict #1:

Steps:

Conflict #2:

Steps:

Intimate relationships are necessary for our health and our spirit. We need to know we are cared for, and we need to care for someone. Not all relationships are or should be intimate, but some have the potential to become immensely satisfying and fulfilling—that warm, comfortable and loving place we all want to be. Those deserve our care and commitment. And we deserve the intimacy.

PERSONAL LIFE MANAGEMENT PLAN STEP #10

Know Yourself

Follow the Rules

Be Persistent

UNIT IV PROGRESS CHECK AND AFFIRMATION

Dear Reader:

You've now gone beyond skills to building the kinds of relationships that bring you real joy in your life. You understand your role in nurturing yourself and in contributing responsibly to relationships. This is an empowering experience.

The insights that you have gained in this unit open up areas in your heart and mind that you may have only dreamed about before. And, these areas have become a new operating style in all of your interactions with others.

A beneficial effect of this process that you are probably noticing by now is the inner comfort and serenity you are starting to feel. This inner core of success becomes a well from which all other success flows. It provides a basis for more growth and self-development.

But for now, affirm your progress, savor your successes, and enjoy your relationships. Say to yourself, "I feel good about how far I have come toward my goals. I am pleased with the new way I am relating to myself and to others!"

We are delighted that you have persisted this far. You have shown dedication and care. A pat on the back to *you*!

Sincerely,

B. W. and S. Mc.

STAGE FIVE: IMPLEMENT PERSONAL AND PROFESSIONAL PLAN

11 Achieving Professional Growth

You have, up to now in this book, looked at life management primarily in a personal vein: how to make changes, how to solve problems, how to maintain and enhance relationships. In the area of your career, the principles are the same, even though they may be applied differently.

You might feel like you are just not happy in a job. Or worse, that you feel a sense of struggle, like you are not in the right place. Maybe you are not going anywhere. Perhaps you are just looking at the beginning of your job path. Whatever stage of your career life you are in now, there is one universal truth: **You spend most of your waking hours pursuing work. If your job does not contribute to your life in a meaningful way, then you are missing a great source of personal fulfillment.** The examples below illustrate the point.

Jemal hates his job at the car manufacturing plant. But, since he makes $18 per hour, he feels he would be foolish to leave. Melaney is an insurance claims representative. Her job is to process client claim forms. Though she is paid well and is well-liked by the people she works with, she feels like her job has no real value.

Both of these people are unhappy with their current career paths. Neither seems to know what to do about this struggle. Being unhappy, or maybe even just not being terribly fulfilled, often does not motivate someone to make changes. Occasionally, it takes being laid off or fired to cause someone to really examine the reason behind working.

Lack of fulfillment or fear of the loss of a job are only two of the dangers of work or career problems. Stress and a sense of struggle, of just not being in the right place, all of these are symptoms of a poor match of job and employee. Work-related stresses invariably spill over into personal life and can affect families and can even harm personal health. So, problems with work life do not just stay at work.

Where are you now? As you have seen in prior chapters, **understanding your current situation is the beginning of change.**

Perhaps you have just decided to move to a new job, to a college education, to a different, more lucrative or satisfying career path. Wherever you are at this moment, you can use career management to guide you toward the most reward in your work. Career management is a careful process of discovery and design—discovery of what you really need in a career, and design of the job that will bring you the most satisfaction.

The beginning point for designing a meaningful career path is to explore the attitudes you have developed over time about working. In the activity below you will be asked to begin a careful examination of what work and a career mean to you.

Assessment Activity # 1

Answer the questions below about your attitudes toward work. Where possible, give an example to explain your answer.

1. What impression do you have of your parents' work? Do they enjoy it? Do they think it is important? Is it just a way to earn money?

2. What experiences have you had with work? Do you work now? Have you worked in the past? Was it a positive experience? What is your strongest impression about it overall?

3. Describe what a good job would be for you.

Dwayne was referred to me because he was experiencing stress at work. He was absent more than other workers, and he seemed to have a lot of conflict with his co-workers as well as his boss. Though competent at what he did, he showed no enthusiasm for his duties. As a medical technician, he did testing and evaluating tasks in a lab.

The first question I asked him when he told me about his job was, "If you didn't have anything standing in your way, what job would you really want to do?" His answer was immediate. "I want to work with patients more and be treated like a real professional." Eventually, it came out that Dwayne wanted to be a nurse, but with a family to support, he didn't feel he could stop earning an income long enough to complete a nursing program.

Feeling trapped, Dwayne had become more and more frustrated with his job. He had become convinced that he had no choices in his current situation. What about you? As you look at what you do every day, would you make any changes? I know, change is a tough choice. But viewing your work as a set of choices that will lead you closer to happiness can give you a sense of freedom and joy.

Now, in the activity below you will be exploring what you really need from the work that you do.

Assessment Activity #2

If you didn't have to worry about the amount of money you earned, what kinds of activities could you enjoy doing on a daily basis? Feel free to put anything (legal) that you like. Often there are ways to turn these values into income-producing activities.

I would enjoy:

I would enjoy:

I would enjoy:

I would enjoy:

If in this activity you put a job name or title, you may be limiting your thinking. There may be a work area that will suit you but doesn't even exist yet. The world of work is changing all the time, so try to keep your thoughts open. Instead of a job name, you might write down a set of conditions you would ideally work within. Here is an example.

Not: "I would like to be a lawyer." But: "I would like a job where I get to analyze problems and research the answers to those problems. I would also like to be respected for my ability to do my job well. I would like to be able to work with people (or alone). I would like to share ideas with other people in the same type of work."

Or you might have a different view of work: "I would like to build something, to plan and carry out a project and be able to see the final result. I would like to be responsible for creating something that other people could look at and I could take pride in having built."

Now that you are thinking more broadly, you might need more room to describe the work you would prefer. Write your new career requirements in the Activity space below.

Assessment Activity #3

Write a description of your ideal work in terms of the conditions you need to make you happy in what you do.

I need in my work:

I need in my work:

I need in my work:

I need in my work:

When Dwayne and I did this exercise, he mentioned several key issues. He had a strong need to work with people and to make a difference in their lives. He also needed the mental stimulation of solving problems and coordinating complex activities. But he still didn't see how he could achieve his nursing goal right away. So, we pursued other ways in which he could meet his needs while keeping his current job. Eventually, he ended up in a task team that developed a plan for technicians to be more closely involved with patients.

Dwayne found a way to achieve his professional goals within his current position. Some people find it necessary to take another approach. Lucy was a 15-year sales veteran with a major telecommunications company. She consistently got good bonuses for her sales and was highly respected at all levels in her company. The company downsized and began offering early retirement buyouts for people who wanted to leave the company voluntarily. Presented with the option of doing something different with her life at the company's expense, she took an opportunity to examine what she really wanted.

After pursuing a college degree in a new area, Lucy is now a physical therapist with a small hospital near where she lives. She describes her current situation as, "What I do every day improves the quality of someone's life. My patients either move, walk, or feel better as a result of what I do. And that matters to me."

Having a place to go for eight hours (or more) a day where you do things that make you feel valued is truly satisfying. **Meaningful work makes individuals feel motivated and enthusiastic every day.** It contributes to high self-esteem, and it nurtures the spirit.

In the **Personal Life Management Plan** guide steps that follow, we will give you a word to help you remember how to chart your career management path. Each letter of the word will stand for one of the steps in the process of developing your career plan. That word is **S–T–R–E–T–C–H.**

Select a goal.

Talk it up to yourself.

Revive your curiosity.

Elevate the goal to a daily priority.

Take advantage of opportunities.

Charge ahead with confidence.

Have a heart.

When you **S–T–R–E–T–C–H** your thinking, you stretch your potential. **Just by expecting satisfaction from your career path, you are increasing your chances for achieving that satisfaction.**

SELECT A GOAL

The first consideration in pursuing a career that will bring you fulfillment is to determine what work-type activities you like. Dr. Fred Ott of Georgia State University describes the process this way: Your primary goal in considering a career direction is joy. This idea, interestingly enough, is fairly new to our culture. For generations we have been told, "Get a good, steady job and stick with it until retirement." Nothing was ever said about enjoying that job.

Today, however, we are seeing so much stress-related illness that we are beginning to look to the workplace as a likely contributor. When your health is affected by emotional factors, then negative work environments can be a very real threat. Since you have begun the process of looking at your career path in terms of your own satisfaction, you will likely find problems that you will need to deal with. Many of you may have already started this and are now in a new job, or in a college or a training program to make changes.

What will make your changes work for you is good goal setting. A key point to remember is: **The goal should be simple and attainable.**

Some people drown themselves in goal statements that are intimidating in their size and complexity. A very intense law student I know showed me his goal statements. One of them was, "I will pass the bar exam in Texas and be admitted as a junior partner in ABC firm by August 1997 at the salary of $62,000 per year to include a company car and benefits."

On the other hand, a housewife who wished to return to the work force wrote as her goal statement, "I want to increase my accounting skills in order to secure a position where I can feel respected and can experience growth."

What Do You Think?

Because of a restructuring plan, Vaughn's company is offering a cash bonus and retraining program to employees who have had consistently superior ratings on their performance for over three years. The money amounts to a year's salary and two years of benefits as long as the employee is enrolled in education or industry training that could potentially apply to the company. Vaughn has a two-year associates' degree and has been a purchasing agent in an electronics plant for the last three years. He is not interested in becoming an engineer and can't think of a business he would like to start. The program allows an extra $5,000 for employees who enroll in a college degree completion or professional certification program. At 25 he is not ready to leave the company, but he would like the opportunity for growth.

What should Vaughn do?

Your goal might read, "My goal is to discover a position that brings me joy" or "I want to work in a high-tech environment and have decision-making control." Another example might be, "I want a job where I can have time for my family."

PERSONAL LIFE MANAGEMENT SKILL #1
SET A GOAL

From the ideas you used in the prior activities in this chapter, develop a goal statement for yourself. It is okay to have more than one goal, but try to keep your statement simple and direct.

My career goal is:

Now that you have a goal or direction, you are ready to move to the next step:

TALK IT UP TO YOURSELF

Attaining life goals requires commitment and energy. You have to constantly give yourself pep talks to keep your level of enthusiasm high. Nothing important is accomplished without enthusiasm. Others may or may not understand your goal or your wish for the goal to be fulfilled. So, they may not be as supportive as you would like. This is unimportant. **You can be your own supporter. It is your goal, your joy, and you are entitled to feel good about it.**

You can do this by activating your goal in your mind. Use present tense statements such as: "My chosen career path is a source of joy." "I devote effort toward my goal." "My goal is vital and positive." By talking about your goal in terms of your "here and now" thinking, you make that goal part of your present reality.

So many people stop goal activity because they talk themselves into believing that the goal is, after all, not attainable. Your challenge is to keep the self-talk positive whether the day is good or bad, or whether your friends are supportive or not. Your goal has value and merit. Remind yourself of that often.

PERSONAL LIFE MANAGEMENT SKILL #2
TALK IT UP TO YOURSELF

Write below things you can say to yourself about your goal that will keep you enthusiastic. Don't forget: It is okay to talk to yourself in the mirror about your potential. Many of the most successful people do it every day.

My goal is valuable because:

____

____

____

My attitude about my goal is:

____

____

____

Talking to yourself in a positive way helps to keep you motivated in the face of all sorts of barriers to your goal-directed activity. Another support for your goal-directed efforts is adding new information and ideas to your mental library.

REVIVE YOUR CURIOSITY

Learning is a part of the success of any new activity. You must learn new skills and information to be able to progress in your life or your job. To do this, you might look at the style of the real experts on learning: children. Children live to learn and savor every new idea and experience because of their natural curiosity.

Ways children are curious include the "Why is it. . . . ?" questions. They want to know how a fire truck works, why the sky has clouds, where the moon goes in the daytime. By being curious, children learn about their world.

You have the same opportunity. When you see people who appear to be doing the type of job you think you would like, you can ask them how they like their work. Or if you see an article on the field you are interested in, you can read about what others have to say. **Curiosity is asking questions, wondering about issues, exploring ideas. It stretches the imagination. It makes "What if . . . ?" become real.**

Reviving curiosity may take some effort, but the returns are tremendous.

But you must discover that information by asking questions. By stimulating your curiosity, you will begin to notice more things that might help you progress on your career path.

PERSONAL LIFE MANAGEMENT SKILL #3
REVIVE YOUR CURIOSITY

Since most adults are a little rusty on this, we will do a warm-up activity.

Warm-up: Look at something in the room where you are right now. Think of three questions you might ask about that object.

Example: There is a clock in the room.

Question 1: How does it work?

Question 2: Who invented clocks?

Question 3: Why are most clocks round?

Now, think about your career goal and come up with some questions that may lead to new ideas that will bring you closer to your goal.

Question 1:

Question 2:

Question 3:

Question 4:

Now that your curiosity has been stimulated, you are beginning to find out what is required to reach your goal. Maybe schooling, training, or new experiences are needed. Whatever you need to do, you must elevate the goal to a daily priority.

ELEVATE YOUR GOAL TO A DAILY PRIORITY

Philip and Adrienne wanted to be in business for themselves, but they had heard that over half of new businesses fail. So, they were curious to find out the reasons for this high failure rate. They went to seminars, read articles in magazines, and talked to small business owners. What they learned is that most people who go into business know their product or service well, but know nothing about managing and marketing a business.

Their curiosity leads to a guide for meeting their goal. One thing they must do to achieve their dream is to learn more about business management and marketing. So, their goal now has sub-goals that they can do one at a time. If they are serious about what they want to do, they will spend some time each day adding to their business knowledge. The next step in your professional S–T–R–E–T–C–H is to elevate your goal to a daily priority.

PERSONAL LIFE MANAGEMENT SKILL #4
ELEVATE YOUR GOAL

From the information you have gathered through your curiosity, pick one of the elements needed for you to reach your career goal. Then, list one or more activities related to this element that you can spend some time on each day.

Element 1:

Activity:

Time schedule for activity:

Element 2:

Activity:

Time schedule for activity:

Once you move your goal *ideas* to the status of goal *actions* you are well on your way to success. **Daily action reinforces you in your quest by directing your energies regularly toward your desired end result.** In addition to this daily activity, you will become more alert to situations that might expose you to opportunities.

TAKE ADVANTAGE OF OPPORTUNITIES

The best advice I can give to someone who wants to move forward in life is this: "Be in the room." Of course this sounds a bit cryptic, but the following situation will explain. A business acquaintance of mine tells this story.

> A year ago I was looking for a way to supplement my income while the children were still at home. We needed the money, and my husband's pay made the bills but did little else. My neighbor told me she was going to a "Women in Business" workshop and invited me along. Though I hesitated at first, I went just out of curiosity. At the end of the day my neighbor and I had gotten enough information to start our own housecleaning business. Today, I have four other women working with me, and I make more than my husband! But I would never have made the step if I had not attended the workshop.

Information on your goal and how to get there is available. The opportunity would have gone unnoticed if the person had not been "in the room." In addition, if she had been in the room and not aware of the potential of what was being discussed, nothing of benefit would have occurred. You are in the middle of a world of opportunity each day. By knowing what factors will bring you closer to your goal, you can tune in to those events, people, and situations that will be helpful to you. A key to this process, though, is getting out and into new "rooms."

Dennis Waitley, a noted motivational speaker, advised me once that the way to get into the career you want is to **be around people that do the particular job you are interested in.** He recommended professional organizations as well as seminars conducted by leaders in the industry. Association with these professionals can create opportunities and expand your knowledge.

PERSONAL LIFE MANAGEMENT SKILL #5
TAKE OPPORTUNITY

Write below circumstances which could create career path opportunities for you. Remember that workshops, trade shows, civic clubs, college courses, seminars, and committees all hold great potential for you. Note: Be as specific as possible. Not "I will go to a trade show" but "I will attend the Franchise Fair in October."

Opportunity 1:

Contribution this will make to my career path:

Opportunity 2:

Contribution this will make to my career path:

Opportunity 3:

Contribution this will make to my career path:

Motivational speakers will tell you that the only bad idea is one that you do not act on or that you dismiss because you think you can't make it happen. **Finding opportunity is helpful, but acting on opportunity is what moves you closer to where you want to be.** If you charge ahead with confidence, then your path will often clear for you.

CHARGE AHEAD WITH CONFIDENCE

If you've smelled a dog that has happened onto a skunk, you know the implications of charging ahead foolishly. On the other hand, fear of the unknown, even if it might turn out to be quite good, stops many from charging at all. One thing you should do for yourself is to build confidence in your goal activities. You do this by engineering successes along the way.

On the way to your final goal of a fulfilling career position are many small goals that need to be accomplished. As you define these goal steps, it helps to make each one small enough so that you can complete it successfully in a limited amount of time. Few people achieve great things by huge leaps; more often they win little victories as they go. These little victories reinforce a clear sense of purpose.

Kent was an intern from a university in his third year of undergraduate school. His parents sent him to me because he had lost direction and was thinking of quitting school. When I asked him why he was in college, he replied, "I don't know anymore because I don't know what I want to do when I get out." He needed some work on his goal setting.

As a botany major he enjoyed his classes, but couldn't see himself as a professor. He was a very outdoorsy type and loved studying the plants and reporting his findings. After we went through the goal-setting activities and curiosity exercises, he decided that he would like to work for a company that monitored the environmental effects of disasters, such as hurricanes, oil spills, and pollution. He had found a goal. To get there, however, he learned that he must obtain a master's degree and gain work experience. After learning this, he stopped again, overwhelmed by the immense barrier of a lengthy educational process.

To motivate him I suggested that he write down a few tasks that he could do in the next week or so that would help him move toward his final goal. He reported to me a week later that he had attended a press conference on environmental impacts and had spoken to one of the people involved with a wetlands research project. From this contact he had found out about a summer internship position. He was beginning to learn how to charge ahead toward success.

For you to do the same thing is quite easy. Here are the guidelines:

1. Set short-term, intermediate goals that are small and relatively easy.
2. Acknowledge your successes as they occur.
3. Affirm your progress often.

Accumulating small successes will give you the confidence to move forward and face the challenge of the larger steps. Successful action leads to more attempts and more successes. With many successes to your credit, temporary barriers or stalls to your goal activity will seem insignificant.

PERSONAL LIFE MANAGEMENT SKILL #6
CHARGE AHEAD

Starting in the space below, begin a log of your completed short-term goals and the date they were successfully completed.

Short-term goal:

Date reached:

Way this leads to the successful completion of my long-term goal:

(Note: This is the format for creating your own success log, so you can chart your progress regularly.)

In your confident charge toward your career path of fulfillment, you must be cautious that you maintain balance. The people you care about are affected by your decisions and choices as well. Personal goals that are harmful to others bring negative long-term results in your life. You must have a clear vision of your goal, but you must also have a heart.

HAVE A HEART

Terence was a restaurant owner in a large city. His wife initially came to me for family therapy because the children were having problems in school. It seemed to the family, she said, that Terence was preoccupied with his dream of opening a second restaurant. Consequently, the children rarely saw their father unless they went to his restaurant. In this case ,Terence's goal activity was succeeding, but at the risk of damage to his family.

The solution in Terence's case was to work with him on including his family in his goal plans. He realized that there were things he wanted to accomplish with his children and his wife as well as with his business.

Admittedly, it is easy to get lost in the pursuit of success, especially if things are going well. But, **personal relationships sustain us far more profoundly than professional accomplishments ever can.** It is a sad case, indeed, when a person begins to see work as the sole source of joy or achievement.

Achievement does require sacrifice, but sacrificing those you love for the sake of a goal may lead to an empty victory. Those who say it's lonely at the top may well have alienated friends and family along the way. This is just not necessary. Some of the most successful and busiest people in the world fiercely protect their family time and priorities.

You will have to make your own decisions about how you want to allocate your time. But, if you include those closest to you in your goal setting and in the steps along the way, you will find a solid support base. When they understand what you are trying to obtain and where they fit into the picture, they will be your biggest fans. Also, by including them in the process, you will prevent their feeling threatened or left out of your life.

PERSONAL LIFE MANAGEMENT SKILL #7
HAVE A HEART

Return to your plan for achieving your goal. Identify ways in which those closest to you can participate in your plan and write them in the space below.

Step 1.

Way others can participate:

Step 2.

Way others can participate:

Step 3.

Way others can participate:

Step 4.

Way others can participate:

Others' goals and needs have value just as yours do. To maintain connections with other people, you will be required to give and take in all areas of your life. The ability to do this will make you a successful life manager.

PERSONAL LIFE MANAGEMENT PLAN STEP #11

Select a Goal

Talk It Up To Yourself

Revive Your Curiosity

Elevate the Goal To a Daily Priority

Take Advantage of Opportunities

Charge Ahead with Confidence

Have a Heart

12

Implementing Your Personal Life Management Plan

Now that you've come this far, look at a picture of your **Personal Life Management Plan:**

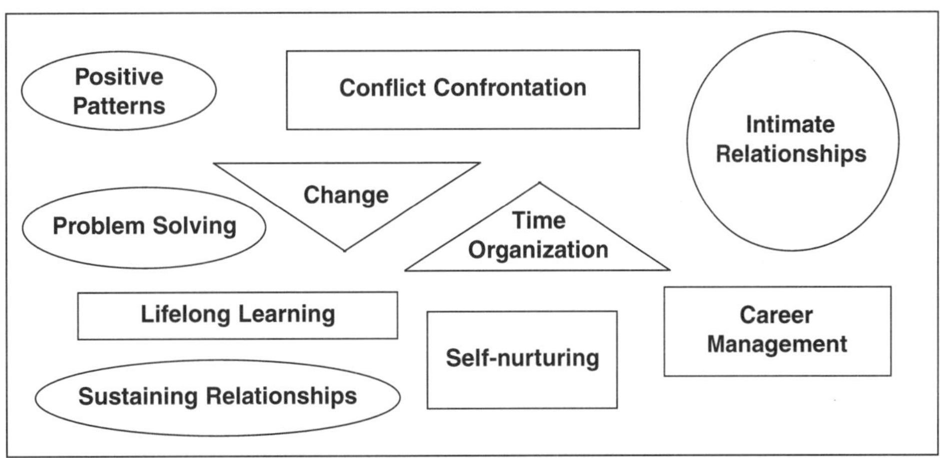

As you can see, your plan has many shapes and sizes in it. These are the different areas you have chosen to address in your life. While you have been developing your plan, you have been changing your operating style. No doubt you are seeing positive results in your personal and professional life.

It is time now to pull together the many parts that you have been working on separately and make a cohesive, solid strategy for continuing your self-development. What you will be doing in this chapter is incorporating your individually selected areas of change into a total framework for life management. There are several steps to this process of tying together, or integrating, your plan so far.

IMPLEMENTING YOUR PLANS
PHASE 1

Turn to the pages at the end of each chapter where you have been compiling the individual entries to your **Personal Life Management Plan.** These are the areas you have selected to create the desired changes in your life patterns. Take a moment to review these. You may find that new insights gained from working through each of the chapters has caused your initial priorities to change. This is okay because growth has taken place and expanded your life view, making some aspects appear different than they did at first glance.

Implementation Activity #1

Write down your new priorities for those areas where you might have changed your view. If there are no changes in an area, you can just copy what you had originally. This review will give you a clear vision of what you are accomplishing.

My new priorities are:

1. For my communicating with others:

2. For my skill building:

3. For my relationshps:

4. For my career:

5. Other priorities:

PHASE 2 For this phase you will implement into your daily routine the plans you have developed for yourself. You have been practicing the skills and the relationship development as you have read each chapter. Now, you will be setting priorities towards incorporating all the ideas on a daily basis. This is a natural step because by now you have become used to practicing the individual skills for specific circumstances.

Review your plan on a daily basis and look for ways to pull together the skill areas so that they support each other. Devise practice situations that will allow you to utilize several skills and insights. An example might be to handle a conflict with your child in terms of supportive communication, problem solving, and intimate relationship considerations. The more you actively insert these areas of practice into your day-to-day activities and relationships, the more you will see them as a **whole approach to living.**

Implementation Activity #2

Write below the skills you intend to practice and suggest situations for practicing them in an integrated way.

Skill #1:

Situations:

Skill #2:

Situations:

Skill #3:

Situations:

Set a conscious goal for yourself each day. For example, "Today I will use a minimum of three areas from my plan." Be sure to vary these or add to them each day to ensure that you continue the growth process in each area.

Implementation Activity #3

Write below your implementation goals for a week. Feel free to photocopy this section for your use each week.

Today's date:

Goal for today:

Today's date:

Goal for today:

Today's date:

Goal for today:

Today's date:

Goal for today:

Today's date:

Goal for today:

Today's date:

Goal for today:

Today's date:

Goal for today:

Challenge yourself to expand and polish your new expertise in human relations. For instance, using your conflict and relationship skills with your child or close friends might be one level. But, expanding that application to your boss might be more difficult. Don't let the difficulty of the task frighten you off. Your first attempt might be somewhat awkward, but the more you practice in new situations, the easier these applications will become. Eventually, your positive, empowered responses to all life's challenges will become automatic and will have replaced the old, ineffective responses that made you unhappy.

Implementation Activity #4

Write below the way in which you will challenge yourself with a new implementation.

Today's challenge:

PHASE 3 As with any new venture, you will run into difficulties from time to time. These include: bad days, negative people, and unrealistic expectations. You can move forward in spite of these barriers with the skills you already have.

With a bad day, for example, you can let yourself relax and recognize it as temporary. Some self-nurturing is helpful on days like this. Most importantly, though, let yourself be imperfect. Just getting through a bad day is a victory. After it, you can go back to being consistent in applying your plan.

Implementation Activity #4

When I have a bad day, I will recognize it as a temporary condition; then I will:

____

____

____

____

to help me get through it in a positive way.

Similarly, there will be people whose negativity will attempt to draw you into their own dark views. Recognize the draining effect these people have on your well-being. Detach yourself from the effects of the experience and return to focusing on your positive operating style.

Implementation Activity #5

Fill in the following:

I can expect certain people to react negatively from time to time as I begin to grow and change.

I will reduce the effect these people can have on me by:

____

____

____

____

It is easy, also, to discourage yourself with unrealistic expectations. What you are doing is an evolving process. Your goals take time to accomplish. When you hit a low point and feel discouraged, go back to self-nurturing. Be consistent, not perfect. Remember that four to six weeks are required to make even simple changes become a part of your everyday habits.

Implementation Activity #6

Fill in the following:

I expect my life to go better as I begin to implement the principles I am learning. But, I understand that things take time. When I become discouraged I will:

____

____

____

PHASE 4 Acknowledging your own progress is an important self-development milestone. Being able to congratulate yourself on little successes as well as big successes shows that you have moved to a new level of maturity. Additionally, it shows that you have gained the insight to differentiate between self-nurturing and ego-feeding.

Affirming progress begins with good goal setting. It is easy for you to get lost in worry over how far you still are from your goals. Instead, you should feel affirmed in success over how close you are to achieving the goals you have set. It is also significant to note the great distance you have come from your starting point.

Implementation Activity #7

In each area of your **Personal Life Management Plan** write an affirmation for yourself that strongly supports the success you have achieved so far. For example:

"I am a constructive problem solver. An example of this is":

____

____

____

____

____

"I cultivate relationships that sustain me. An example of this is":

____

____

____

____

____

"I view conflict as a positive experience that helps me understand others. An example where I have had this experience is":

____

____

____

____

____

"I am working in career directions that bring me joy. An example is":

____

____

____

____

____

In the space below write any additional examples that affirm your progress:

____

____

____

____

____

CONTINUING DEVELOPMENT USING YOUR PERSONAL LIFE MANAGEMENT PLAN

Self-development is a lifelong process. It does not stop with a certain birthday or achievement. It is ongoing. Conditions will continue to change, so you will always need new approaches and behaviors. The skills you have learned in this book will apply throughout your life and will help in new situations.

What Do You Think?

A large printing company has just hired you as a new director of training in the human resources department. You have interviewed many employees and managers about problems in the workplace and have come up with the following conclusions:

Morale is low because employees seem to feel that the company doesn't do enough for them. Since people have to work odd shifts, many employees say that their family lives are suffering. There is some evidence of drug abuse in one department. Two managers have not conducted yearly reviews for their employees for raises. The company is being sold, and people are nervous about the outcome. They think things will be different, and they won't have a job anymore.

What seminars or training topics that you have learned in studying this book would you recommend to help the problems in this situation?

At any point, if you find yourself struggling or confused with conditions or relationships in your personal or professional life, you can refer to the model introduced in Chapter 1.

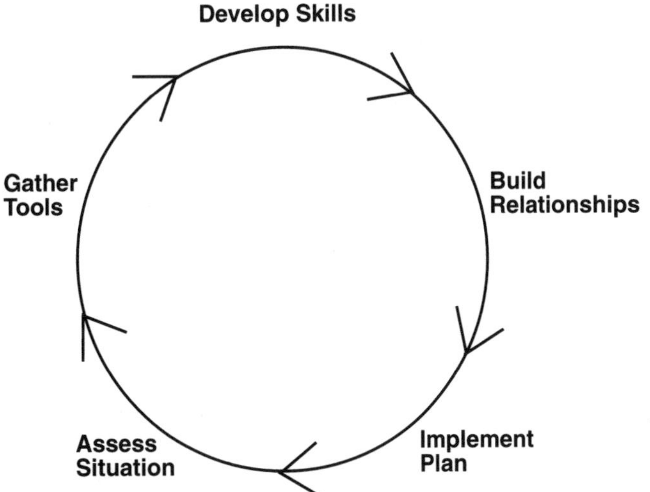

This is the **Personal Life Management Plan** formula for growth just as it appeared in the first chapter. This book has now come full circle, just as you have. You will note, however, that the process can be repeated again and again. Growth is a lifelong endeavor, just as learning and career development are lifelong. This formula will guide you in all aspects of your life. You must, however, provide the force and the direction for change.

PERSONAL LIFE MANAGEMENT PLAN STEP #12

Identify Areas of Work

Develop Daily Goals

Overcome Barriers

Affirm Progress

UNIT V PROGRESS CHECK AND AFFIRMATION

Dear Reader:

You have done it. In spite of all the interruptions, responsibilities, and challenges, you have completed this book. By doing this one act, you have begun a series of events that will ever alter your future. Now, you have learned what you need to know to move on toward the life you want.

In a way you don't need us anymore. If you have followed the guidelines set forth in this book, you are now the commander of your own fate, the driver of your own potential, and the implementer of your life's dreams.

However, if you ever lose your way for a brief time, you can always come back, read a chapter or two, and review your plan.

Tomorrow is yours. May things continue well for you.

Best Wishes,
B.W and S. Mc.

Personal Life Management Plan Summary

Step One: Build the Foundation
- Define your dream

Step Two: Realize Potential Through Change
- Find areas of discomfort
- Make a commitment
- Visualize change
- Practice change behaviors

Step Three: Organize Time and Tasks
- Prioritize necessary track
- Secure resources
- Complete tasks

Step Four: Utilize Lifelong Learning
- Become an active listener
- Use interactive reading

Step Five: Use Constructive Communication
- Eliminate negative talk
- Adopt a constructive style
- Build a positive environment

Step Six: Replace Worry with Problem Solving
- Isolate "real" problem
- Generate solutions
- Weed out least workable
- Implement best solution
- Congratulate yourself

Step Seven: Confront Conflict
- Handle emotions
- Listen to details
- Assert your needs
- Note other's needs
- Focus on issues
- Persist toward mutual solution

Step Eight: Nurture Self
- Care for body needs
- Take a break
- Challenge yourself
- Create privacy
- Manage finances
- Form affiliations

Step Nine: Develop Sustaining Relationships
- Use supportive listening
- Voice needs
- Handle needs conflicts
- Re-think rejection

Step Ten: Cultivate Intimate Relationships
- Know yourself
- Follow the rules
- Be persistent

Step Eleven: Achieve Professional Growth
- Select a goal
- Talk it up
- Revive curiosity
- Elevate priority
- Take opportunities
- Charge ahead
- Have a heart

Step Twelve: Implement Plan
- Identify work areas
- Develop daily goals
- Overcome barriers
- Affirm progress

Note: This summary is to help you keep on track in your **Personal Life Management Plan.** Copy or remove this page and keep it in a convenient place for reference.

This Certifies

____

as a

Personal Life Manager

with all the happiness and success
that accompany that achievement.

Brenda L. Walters
____

Sandra L. McKee
____

Authors

Practice Exercises

INSTRUCTIONS

For each chapter you will be given a case or cases to analyze that reflect the concepts in the chapter. By answering questions you will demonstrate your understanding of the ideas from each chapter.

Chapter 1: The Formula

Exercise #1 Application

Joe has invested in a class to help manage his life better. There is a money-back guarantee on the class, so Joe wants to be sure things are better for him as a result of the class. Help Joe assess the potential of the class for his personal development.

To alter his potential, Joe:

a. Will have to make great and permanent changes in his life.

b. Will not have to learn any new skills.

c. Will have to make only small but permanent changes.

d. Does nothing. He cannot alter his potential.

The main barrier to Joe's achieving his potential is:

a. His wife.

b. Fate.

c. The economy.

d. Joe's own past.

CHAPTER 2: CHANGE

Exercise #1 Application

Danny and his family decided a weekend camping trip would be a welcome change from their usual weekend routine. His parents asked if they could come along. The family agreed. It was midmorning when the family arrived at the campground. The manager had lost Danny's reservation for a camper parking slot that had water and power. So, they had to go to the wilderness camping area with only a restroom for facilities. After setting up, the family decided to unhook the car and drive to the lake for the afternoon. Upon returning, they noticed that one of the tires on the camper was flat. Over the next two days several other mishaps occurred including a broken windshield wiper, sunburn on the two children, and a minor fall by Danny's father. Danny's wife does crisis management and handles all the problems that have occurred. Danny, on the other hand, has screamed at the tire, yanked the wiper off the car, and sworn never to go camping with the family again.

What is Danny's attitude toward unexpected events?

a. He welcomes them as opportunities to grow and change.

b. He feels like he must be cursed.

c. He acts in a positive and constructive manner.

d. He demonstrates his resilience in the face of the unexpected.

What would a resilient response to Danny's situation be?

a. Yell and swear.

b. Blame his Dad for not preparing the camper better.

c. Understand that things happen and find some humor in them.

d. Whine and sulk.

CHAPTER 3: TIME MANAGEMENT

Exercise #1 Application

Janeice has a calendar on the wall of her kitchen that holds the dates and times of all the activities her family is involved in. She breaks her week down into responsibility time and free time. She plans outings for the kids on the weekends and never forgets to send a card for a relative's birthday.

Janeice's thinking style is:

a. Quick, creative thinking.

b. Careful, methodical.

c. Crazy.

d. Quick, planner.

She likely will be stressed by problems that:

a. Do not have a known procedure for solving.

b. Are orderly and fit into a pattern.

c. Are presented to her in a clear, organized way.

d. None of these are stressors.

CHAPTER 4: LIFELONG LEARNING

Exercise #1 Application

Two friends, Randy and Josh, wrote several songs for their band to perform when they played nightclubs. They thought it was nice to have some original music. At one of their performances a record producer approached them about cutting a demonstration record in her studio using one of their songs. She asked, "Have you copyrighted your songs?" Randy and Josh had never thought about doing that, so they realized they had better find out more about the business end of the music business.

Where would they *least* likely find information about copyrighting?

a. A coffeehouse which guitarists are known to frequent.

b. An attorney.

c. A book in the library about copyrighting music.

d. The state songwriter's association.

CHAPTER 5: CONSTRUCTIVE COMMUNICATION

Exercise #1 Application

Manuel is excited about his first job out of high school. On the first day he met an older worker who was instructed to "show him the ropes." When the supervisor left the room, the worker told Manuel, "Look kid, this is the way it is. You don't do too much around here and you don't suck up to the supervisor because it makes the rest of us look bad."

Manuel's reaction to this "advice" should be:

a. Agree with the worker and adopt the attitude he suggests.
b. Respond with, "Yeah, this is a rotten job anyway."
c. Tell the supervisor what the worker said.
d. Recognize the negative talk and maintain his positive attitude.

Manuel will have to do what to keep his attitude good?

a. Stay away from "gloom and doom" people on the job.
b. Ask the worker why he feels the way he does.
c. Try not to take seriously the "down" talk from this worker.
d. All the above.

CHAPTER 6: PROBLEM SOLVING

Exercise #1 Application

Lora is a retired transit worker. Her husband, Emil, has a carpet business in which he is very involved. Because of a slump in building, Emil is making less money than he used to. Without Lora's additional income, they have had to cut back on some things they enjoy doing. Lora is unhappy and tells Emil that they have a problem in their marriage and the problem is that he's not making enough money.

Identify the "real" problem:

a. Lora feels empty and bored.
b. Lora loves money.
c. Emil is having an affair.
d. Emil is not making enough money.

What would be a good solution to their situation?

a. Take out a loan.
b. Divorce.
c. Think of things they could do together that don't cost much.
d. Lora could have an affair.

CHAPTER 7: CONFLICT

Exercise #1 Application

Ann-li was in her second year of her law practice. Her mother had recently died, and her father insisted on living alone in his home. Ann-li worked 10 to 11 hour days. Her father had begun to call her many times a day about one problem or another, and the calling was beginning to interfere with her work. The senior partner in the law office gently, but firmly, told her that she must make better arrangements. Ann-li was reaching the end of her patience. She felt that her father needed some sort of live-in care because of his severely limiting arthritis, but every discussion about that option ended up in an argument. She wanted to be a good daughter, but her job was being jeopardized. She was angry and felt helpless.

What is the true source of Ann-li's distress?

a. Her father.

b. Her mother's death.

c. Her boss.

d. Her inability to deal with the situation.

What are Ann-li's needs in this situation?

a. She needs to care for her father without interference with her work.

b. She needs a day off.

c. She needs to move in with her father.

d. She needs to get a hobby and forget the problem.

CHAPTER 8: SELF-NURTURING

Exercise #1 Application

A woman I met on the plane recently was experiencing high levels of stress. She was flying home to her family from the city where she worked 500 miles away. She spoke of problems at work, long hours, a general feeling of isolation. We talked about her situation, and she described herself as generally healthy, highly motivated, and serious about her work. Her whole demeanor, though, was one of apparently being stretched to the limit. When I asked her about her reasons for the visit home, she said, "I just need to talk to people who understand me."

What need does this woman have to fill to self-nurture?

a. Challenge self for growth.

b. Care for body needs.

c. Form meaningful affiliations.

d. Manage finances responsibly.

What self-nurturing activity could she do to help meet this need?

a. Eat health foods.

b. Exercise to a video program.

c. Hire an accountant.

d. Join a civic or church group.

CHAPTER 9: SUSTAINING RELATIONSHIPS

Exercise #1 Application

Leona has several close friends. Barbara went to school with Leona and has known her for 14 years. They talk three or four times a year at a traditional lunch get-together. At those lunches they share the trials and the joys of the time since the last lunch. Rarely do they talk in between. Cedric is Leona's office mate at work. They share daily stories about funny or difficult times with their kids. Leona has never met Cedric's wife, nor has Cedric met Leona's husband. Patricia is Leona's "best friend." They share confidences and know everything about each other. Patricia's most recent boyfriend is an abuser. Weekly, Leona receives a phone call from Patricia, crying about her problems, and twice Leona has taken Patricia to the hospital with her injuries. Patricia will not break up with the boyfriend in spite of Leona's advice. She always thanks Leona profusely for her help and says, " I don't know what I would do without you."

Which of Leona's friendships is draining?

a. Cedric.

b. Patricia.

c. Barbara.

d. None—all are sustaining.

Of her sustaining relationships what makes them nurturing?

a. The mutual support.

b. Who pays the lunch tab.

c. They spend time together.

d. One cleans the other's house.

CHAPTER 10: INTIMATE RELATIONSHIPS

Exercise #1 Application

As a junior in college, Leonard thinks he is the world's oldest virgin. His lack of sexual experience bothers him when he listens to the "conquests" of his friends, but he feels strongly about the role of sex in a serious, permanent relationship. He has a close and dear friend, Nimarah. They have been a couple for three years and delight in each other's company. Leonard's roommate, Geoffrey, talks about the women he is "intimate" with, boasting about how often he sleeps with different ones. Leonard finally challenges Geoffrey with , "You don't even know what intimacy is. Sex is not all there is to it." Geoffrey laughs at Leonard and says he doesn't know "what's going on."

From the criteria in the chapter describing intimate relationships, which of the roommates is involved in an intimate relationship?

a. Leonard.

b. Geoffrey.

Which of the following is true of Geoffrey?

a. He understands the idea of "closeness."

b. He understands the idea of "safety."

c. He understands the idea of mutual respect.

d. None of the above.

CHAPTER 11: CAREER MANAGEMENT

Exercise #1 Application

You have a neighbor whose daughter is graduating from high school. She is confused about her future, and your neighbor has asked you to talk to her about the directions she should take.

Your first question to her should be:

a. Why don't you consider modeling as pretty as you are?

b. Aren't you going to marry the Simmer's son?

c. If nothing was in your way, what would you like to do?

d. Why are you worried? Your parents will take care of you.

As you direct her in looking at career and/or college, where would you refer her?

a. To people who are doing what she says she would like.

b. To seminars in subject areas she is interested in.

c. To seek out volunteer or internship positions that relate to her interests.

d. All of the above.

CHAPTER 12: IMPLEMENTING THE PLAN

Exercise #1 Application

Gustave was sitting in his therapist's office. It was his first visit, and he announced to the therapist, "My life is a mess. I don't know what to do anymore." Here is his story. "I'm about to lose my job because I had an argument with my supervisor, and I really lost control. I don't know what happened to me; I'm not usually like that. Things have been tough at work lately, and my wife is yelling at me for working late all the time. I don't know how to tell my boss I need to leave at five when we are so far behind. And I sure hate fighting with my wife. We used to get along so well, but now we hardly ever pass a kind word between us. I just can't take it anymore."

What skill is Gustave *most* lacking in?

a. Change management.

b. Time management.

c. Positive communication.

d. Conflict management.

What should Gustave do for his relationship with his wife?

a. He should assert his need to have his own life.

b. His wife and he need to practice supportive listening.

c. He needs to avoid confrontations with his wife.

d. He should forget about his marital problems and get a hobby.

CAREER PLANNING SUPPLEMENT—BUILDING A RESUME

One instrumental tool in getting the job that starts you on your desirable career path is the well-crafted resume. In this supplement you will find several suggested formats. Each has successfully gotten job seekers to the interview stage. I will try to give you some guidelines to help you select the format best suited for your situation.

Building a resume is done by levels. These levels parallel the levels of attention of the reader. If your resume is the commercial for the product (you), then it must be constructed with the goal of getting your reader to tune into what you have to offer. Each level of the resume must hold the potential employer's interest and pull him or her into the next level.

LEVEL I

To start, you should have an attractive visual effect. Cheap paper and a type font that looks like an old typewriter does not impress anyone. If you do not do word processing, you will have to pay someone to dress up the type for you. So many people nowadays have access to desktop publishing and other word processing that employers expect a classy visual effect. Your resume will be passed over and not even read if it looks hastily done or poorly presented. There is no need to get too fancy, unless you are applying for a job in art or advertising. But neat and well-organized resumes do have an advantage.

Ann Allyson
406 Chadburn Ferry Road
Wierton, WV 57930
(406) 555-0095

LEVEL II Match who and what you are professionally with the specific job needs of a prospective employer. At one time, job seekers would include a "Job Objective" section. But these are often too general to be helpful to a potential employer or too specific to keep doors open for the job seeker. Try beginning with a Professional Capabilities section instead.

Professional Capabilities: Problem solving and strong communication skill demonstrated in a customer-oriented environment. Computer capabilities in LOTUS and several word-processing softwares. Maturity and stability in work situations.

Remember that in this section you should represent yourself as you want the employer in your chosen area to view you. Thus, your capabilities section might read differently.

Professional Capabilities: Electronics trouble-shooter trained in board-level diagnostics and familiar with field testing techniques. Have worked with network systems. Experience handling customers in a technical setting.

LEVEL III By this point the reader is probably interested or not, depending on the job needs of the company. Rarely does a reader look at a very general professional capabilities section and try creatively to think of a place to use your skills. You must word the above section to fit jobs you think are available. The same is true in the middle section where you list all the things you have done.

For older, more experienced job seekers, a functional approach, describing what you have accomplished and how long you have been gaining skill in a particular line of work, might be best. This would be done as line items.

FORMAT A

Employment Highlights:
- Implemented client-server software system for twelve-station local area network.
- Supported software programs as technical service representative for national accounts for major accounting software company.
- Demonstrated and conducted training on LOTUS in customer settings.

For less experienced people, or those embarking on a new career with mostly education to recommend them, a "managed page" approach is best. When people scan a resume, they generally lose concentration about two-thirds of the way down the page and are thinking about turning the page instead of focusing on what they are reading. In addition, those with little work history related to the job they are seeking seldom can impress a potential employer with their wealth of experience. So, the strategy is to direct the eye of the reader to those elements of your qualifications that fit the sought-after job.

This strategy includes putting high on the page achievements in school (recent achievements, not years before), honors in military or civic/professional organizations, course work during college or grade point average. In addition, this strategy uses a skills section that will show all the many talents and skills you have in a way that will impress the reader.

FORMAT B

Boylan Anderson
2500 Lake Vista Drive
West Palm Beach, FL 33476

Education: Associate of Applied Science Degree
Graduation June 1996 Major: Health Administration
Hills and Valleys Community College
GPA–3.8 out of 4.0

Accomplishments: Supported self 100% through school, member of National Honor Fraternity, Vice President of Toastmasters

Skills:

Software	*Hardware*
LOTUS 1-2-3	IBM 486
Word for Windows	LCD (for presentations)

By this point the reader is beginning to pay less attention to a line by line scrutiny of your resume. But, if he or she has seen something desirable, then there will be motivation to continue through your work history. Remember, this format is used when you have little or no actual work experience in the field for which you are applying. You are pulling desirable and employable features about yourself into the most visible portions of the resume, "putting your best foot forward" so to speak.

Another format for this level of the resume is the classic "Work History" section. In this, you list your past jobs chronologically—from most recent to most distant. If you have worked only a few years, you might do well to use the format immediately above and add a work history section afterwards. You might have had a series of part-time jobs while in school, so your history might look erratic or undefined. If this is the case, you might want to sum up this time by saying, "Part-time jobs while supporting self through college included: fast food, teaching assistant, and retail clerk."

If you have gaps in your work history from layoffs, illness, or other reasons, the functional resume, Format A above, is the best to sell your strengths before you have to explain why you were not employed for intervals of time. As a general format a chronological work history looks like this:

FORMAT C

Employment History:

March 1994–Present Carpenter
Produced estimates for home-building projects from plans. Worked with customers on ensuring satisfaction with plans and all aspects of construction. Supervised crews.

June 1991–March 1994 Auto sales
Continually met quotas for sales to fleet managers.

The final sections can include whatever you deem desirable, whether it is professional organizations or achievements, awards, civic clubs, hobbies, or willingness to travel and/or relocate. Every resume should have a "References" section, it seems, but interestingly enough, most sources recommend that you put "References available upon request." Of course you will have people in mind who have already agreed to say positive things about you. It is important to get the permission of those you submit as references. When I am asked to recommend someone, I only agree for those I feel I can strongly and positively support. Don't press people into agreeing. If they turn you down, it is probably because they don't feel they know you well enough to answer questions from a potential employer.

This is by no means a definitive discussion of how to produce a winning resume. There are books and whole classes on the topic. But it will get you started. The guidelines for your effort become your own understanding of how the levels of strategy can be best applied to your situation.

Remember that a resume is an ad for you as a product. You receive about 60 seconds of your potential customer's attention in the reading of your resume. Use strategy to put the good information about you in the most noticeable place. Allow each section to appear uncrowded and it will draw the eye of the reader.

Keep in mind also what you have learned in this chapter. A resume is built to help you eventually command the job that will bring you joy. It is a documentary of the choices you have made on your career path and an introduction to the professional you wish to be.

Suggested Reading

Brammer, Lawrence M. *How To Cope with Life Transitions: The Challenge of Personal Change.* New York: Hemesphere Publishing Corp, 1991.

Coleman, James Covington. *Success in College.* Chicago: Foresman, 1960.

Covey, Steven. *First Things First.* New York: Fireside Books, 1994.

DeAngelis, Barbara. *Confidence: Finding It and Living It.* Carson, CA: Hay House.

Douglas, Merrill F., and Donna N. Douglas. *Manage Your Time, Manage Your Work, Manage Yourself.* New York: Amacom, 1980.

Dyer, Wayne. *The Sky's the Limit.* New York: Pocket Books, 1980.

Faya, Allen. *Success with People.* Upper Saddle River, NJ: Prentice Hall, 1995.

Fishbein, Morris. *Successful Marriages.* New York: Doubleday, 1963.

Fulgum, Robert. *From Beginning to End.* Toronto, Canada: Random House, 1995.

Hendrix, Harville. *Keeping the Love You Find.* New York: Pocket Books, 1992.

Krueger, David W. *Success and Fear of Success in Women.* New York: Free Press, 1994.

Mackenzie, Alec. *The Time Trap.* New York: Amacom, 1990.

McKay, Matthew, and Patrick Fannery. *Self-Esteem.* Oaklin, CA: New Harbinger, 1992.

Odlorne, George. *The Change Resister.* Englewood Cliffs, NJ: Prentice Hall, 1981.

O'Grady, Dennis. *Taking the Fear Out of Change.* Hollbrook, MA: Bob Adams, 1992.

Reilly, William John. *Successful Human Relations.* New York: Harper, 1952.

Robbins, Anthony. *Unlimited Power.* New York: Fawcett Columbine, 1986.

Roberts, Ken. *A Rich Man's Secret.* St. Paul, MN: Llewellyn Publishing, 1995.

Seegelman, Ellen. *Personal Risk: Mastering Change in Love and Work.* New York: Harper and Row, 1983.

Seligmen, Martin, Ph.D. *Learned Optimism.* New York: Pocket Books, 1990.

Tarr, Graham. *The Management of Problem-solving, Positive Results from Productive Thinking.* New York: Halsted Press, 1973.

Wieder, Marcia. *Making Your Dreams Come True.* New York: Mastermedia Limited, 1993.

Wolter, Dwight. *Forgiving Our Parents.* Mineapolis, MN: CompCare Publishers, 1988.